The Selfless Self

The Selfless Self

LAURENCE FREEMAN

A Medio Media Book

Continuum • New York

1998
The Continuum Publishing Company
370 Lexington Avenue
New York, NY 10017

Printed in the United States of America
Library of Congress Cataloging-in-Publication Data

Freeman, Laurence.
    The selfless self / Laurence Freeman.
        p.   cm.
    "A Medio Media book."
    ISBN 0–8264–1091–X
    1. Meditation – Christianity.   I. Title.
BV4813.F74   1998
248.3′4–dc21   98-52980
                                                                          CIP

Contents

Contents

How to Meditate

Sit down. Sit still and upright. Close your eyes lightly. Sit relaxed but alert. Silently, interiorly begin to say a single word. We recommend the prayer-phrase "maranatha." Recite it as four syllables of equal length. Listen to it as you say it, gently but continuously. Do not think or imagine anything – spiritual or otherwise. If thoughts and images come, these are distractions at the time of meditation, so keep returning to simply saying the word. Meditate each morning and evening for between twenty and thirty minutes.

The World Community for Christian Meditation

Meditation creates community. Since the first Christian Meditation Centre was started by John Main in 1975, a steadily growing community of Christian meditators has spread around the world. Individual meditators frequently begin to meet in small weekly groups and the network of these groups provides wider support and encouragement for those who wish to sustain their daily practice of morning and evening meditation.

The groups meet in homes, parishes schools, prisons, business, religious communities and government departments. Beginning with a short teaching on meditation, often drawn from the Community's collection of taped talks by John Main, the group then meditates together in silence for half an hour. After the talk, there is time for discussion. The groups are by nature ecumenical and practice an open-door hospitality, welcoming anyone who comes sincerely seeking silence.

A growing number of Christian Meditation Centres, some residential, others located in meditators' homes, also serve to communicate the way of silence taught in this tradition. The Centres help co-ordinate the local weekly groups and organize regular retreats, seminars and other meditation events.

The International Centre in London co-ordinates this world-wide community of meditators. A quarterly newsletter, giving spiritual teaching and reflection, is sent out from London and distributed from a number of national centers, together with local and international news of retreats and other events being held in the world-wide community. An annual John Main Seminar is held in Europe and North America on alternate years.

This Centre is funded entirely by donations and especially through a Friends of the International Centre programme.

The World Community for Christian Meditation
International Centre
23 Kensington Square
London W8 5HN
United Kingdom
Tel: 44 171 937 4679 Fax: 44 171 937 6790
E-mail: wccm@compuserve.com

Visit The World Community for Christian Meditation Web site for information, weekly mediation group reading and discussion at: **www.wccm.org**

United States: Christian Meditation Centre / 1080 West Irving Park Rd. / /Roselle, IL 60172.
Tel/Fax: 1 630 351 2613

John Main Institute / 7315 Brookville Rd. / Chevy Chase, MD 20815.
Tel: 1 301 652 8635
E-mail: wmcoerp@erols.com

Christian Meditation Centre / 1619 Wright St. / Wall, NJ 07719.
Tel: 1 732 681 6238 Fax: 1 732 280 5999
E-mail: gjryan@aol.com

The Cornerstone Centre / 1215 East Missouri Ave. / Suite A 100 / Phoenix, AZ 85014-2914.
Tel: 1 602 279 3454 Fax: 1 602 957 3467
E-mail: ecrmjr@worldnet.att.net

Introduction

In this book I am talking about silence: an inherently contradictory activity. In fact an absurd enterprise, unless the words point to an experience of silence and encourage us to enter silence for ourselves rather than just thinking or talking about it.

The emphasis on the priority of experience lies at the heart of John Main's teaching and the growing influence that teaching has had around the world since his death in 1982. Only a few years earlier, in 1977, John Main had founded the Benedictine Priory of Montreal, a community of monks and lay-people centred on the practice of meditation in the Christian tradition and committed to sharing it with Christians and those of other faiths or of no faith.

An essential feature of this community was the meditation groups that came to meet at the priory on certain evenings for a talk on meditation and then to meditate together. That practice has continued, and the chapters of this book are drawn from talks given to people who have come to the monastery after their day's work. Immediately after each talk we enter the experience of meditation together. The words point to silence.

Many modern people have a spiritual thirst and hunger for silence, for interiority, and for prayer that is as urgent in its way as the material needs of the developing nations. Indeed, unless the spiritual health of the affluent is restored through spiritual experience they will be unable to feel the true compassion from which the love of peace and justice springs. Modern people need a way to return to this health, a way that must be new and old: a traditional way that meets people where they are.

John Main's rediscovery and development of the Christian tradition of meditation, and his insight into the simplicity and poverty of the mantra, have shown such a way to innumerable people. It is a way that excludes no other ways. But it can unite the infinite variety of human ways of being in the Spirit. To sit down in silence and stillness, to repeat the mantra in simple faith throughout the meditation period each morning and evening: this is a discipline and a way to liberty. It is not a panacea. It is a way to live the mystery of life, its griefs and joys, in faith and with the power of faith that heals and raises the human being to love of God and neighbour. It is practical. It is absolutely simple. It unites generations, races and creeds.

The message of these talks is simple: choose a quiet place each morning and evening to step aside from the activities of life. Sit still and simply be. Do not follow your thoughts but 'set your mind on the kingdom before everything else'. The faithful repetition of a word sacred in your tradition, throughout these periods of stillness, will lead you to silence. An ideal Christian word, which John Main warmly recommended, is '*Maranatha*', spoken slowly and rhythmically, 'ma-ra-na-tha'. It is an ancient Christian prayer, in Aramaic, meaning 'Come, Lord'.

In the depth of recited prayer we soon come to experience the real nature of silence. It is not merely the absence of sound-waves. It is the simple, unpretentious nature of things and people as they are in themselves. Nature is silent because it is not pretending to be anything but what it is, nor is it even trying to communicate. A cliff, a tree, the sea is untranslatable. By being what it is, it establishes communion; and by our accepting it and respecting it, we come to the contemplation of nature that leads us to reverence it as created by God. In silence, in being ourselves in the present moment, we move from the contemplation of nature to the contemplation of God and we realise a harmony with God, humanity and nature.

When we are simply ourselves, we are silent. Meditation is the path of silence because it leads us to accept and revere our essential nature. We are not pretending or posing or communicating. If we can come to this silence, we discover that we share human nature in common with every person on the planet.

Our world, our cities, our places of education, of debate, of healing, of administration and manufacturing, need silence: not to escape the realities of our problems, but to encounter the common reality of human nature and communion with what it reflects and seeks to worship.

This is the message of religion before it loses contact with silence and the contemplative experience. When religions become like advertisements for themselves, humanity loses its main hope for the peace that is inseparable from unity.

The tradition that John Main revived is being lived today by men and women around the world. The people who listened to his words came from a broad spectrum of modern urban living. They knew that their lives lacked the integrating experience of prayer. With that experience restored to our daily lives, we can all be open to the power of compassion that flows from it as we walk down the busiest streets or struggle for air in the noisiest subway.

This book is also about the experience of unity: the unity of all men and women in their essential human nature regardless of race, creed or social position; and the unity of all religions in believing – however much individuals may fail that conviction – that there is an ultimate and benevolent truth, dwelling with us and beyond us, and that love and compassion are its signs as well as the way to find it.

The Christian faith of this book is accordingly placed at the feet of all other religions, at their disposal. Christianity is most itself when it seeks the lowest place at the banquet of world religions rather than the presiding role. The Lord Jesus' kingdom is not of this world; the centre is God not Man. Christ is the patient servant of unity and has made himself one with all.

Wherever there is truth the Word of God is present, because the Word is the sole manifestation of God. If Christ is not in all truth and if all truth is not in Christ, then Christian faith is a dream rather than the prayer that answers itself, that 'they may all be one'.

Meditation realises the hope for unity through silence and by a transformation of human nature. But it is the work of the Spirit in human experience that accomplishes this, and so no technique or method can pull the switch of divinisation or claim supremacy over others. Here is a way of meditation that is ancient, perhaps as ancient as Man's religious consciousness, one that spans East and West and one that has a particular relevance for the people of our complex and volatile world. The mantra leads to silence. In silence all roads join to become the Way, and in the transcendent power of the Spirit the human self becomes selfless.

Christian Meditation Centre
London

LAURENCE FREEMAN
November 1988

Experience, Knowledge and Love

The image of a journey or pilgrimage is a natural one to employ when we think about meditation or about the whole of life. It is a very apt image because reflection on experience reveals constant change and often unpredictable development within something that itself remains the same. The journey is a constant, but within the journey there is continual change.

The real journey is the creation of the person we are. And the person we are becoming is unique but also in union with all others. Here is the mystery of creation – that everything within creation is both unique and united. None of us will ever, can ever, be repeated. Our oneness is an aspect of our Godlikeness and a reason why we must reverence each other, and our own selves, so deeply. Yet there also is the most extraordinary unity in the oneness between ourselves and the human family, and between humanity and all creation. All this infinite uniqueness is somehow ordered, centred and purposeful. The more we live out the journey and discover ourselves, the more we allow life to realise us, the more clearly we contemplate the underlying unity within the whole grand design of creation.

One might, for the sake of understanding, identify three stages of awakening along this journey. Whether these are stages of human development or whether they are parts of the structure of any particular event or period in life does not really matter. At the beginning of the journey it seems that the most important thing for us is to *experience*. We need to experience as much as possible and we go exploring in search of experience, hungry for it, eager for it. At first it is not so important what we experience, so long as we feel that the contents of consciousness are being augmented. The *meaning* will come later. What matters now is that we get the material together. At this stage it is a primarily sensory or material dimension of

1

consciousness that is being awakened and used to awaken the next stage. It is not *bad* but incomplete. The great problem we face at this stage is how can we experience enough. How can we pack everything in? As we begin to realise that we cannot achieve omniscience or be and do everything within the range of human potential, acquisitiveness seems to be the wrong approach. We sense that our hopes for plenitude are doomed to failure at that level and, in reaction, anxiety or depression (a characteristic of this stage of adolescence) can set in.

Gradually, and at the painful cost of our illusions and desires, another dimension of consciousness begins to dawn. We begin to see things from a greater height of detachment and the focus of attention begins to shift from raw experience to integrated *knowledge*. We begin to live more in the mind and to discover the mind's amazing powers as riches. It appears wonderfully as a better tool for mastering reality with greater range and subtlety. So we begin to try to absorb as much knowledge as we can. We become self-conscious learners, students of understanding the data. If we do not try to acquire all the information we can possibly cram in, an amassing of trivia, then we seek the key ideas. We ask what are the master-key ideas that will fit any lock, that will open all the doors to understanding, to truth. With the advent of mutual consciousness in relationship, we are more aware of the nature of reality but we are still susceptible to a lust for ideas, the desire to possess what we love.

Gradually the realisation dawns that the scope of mental knowledge is endless. It is as endless as a circle or as infinite as the reflections of two mirrors facing each other. But the mind's infinity is not eternity, only an image of reality. By encountering our own nature as image, we touch the hem of the cloak of transcendence. We could, if we chose to, remain within this mental consciousness for a lifetime, always discovering new reflections and connections, new points at which to begin the circle until we begin to realise that this is not a satisfying dimension. If we so choose, and yet are also aware of the incompleteness of that dimension of consciousness, the danger is that we become cynical, deniers of absolute truth. If we know this and do not go further we will almost certainly become cynical. The problem for us, knowing the limitations of the mental life, is to know where we go from here? What do we *do*?

If we do not become cynical, the danger is that we withdraw from the impassioned pursuit of truth altogether. We lose heart. We compromise. We say, well, life is about enduring things and getting through and waiting for something to happen. The absolute is a romance. We give up being real pilgrims. We allow ourselves to be carried along, not by the spirit of truth, but by the crowd and social conventions.

This is why it is such a moment of grace, at whatever stage of life it may happen, to discover a spiritual path. For many people it is only at this cooling point that they do recognise the spiritual path beside them. The discovery itself occurs within a mysterious dimension. The very way in which we recognise the spiritual as the culmination of both the sensory and the mental, seems to be the way we have to follow. The door we step through on to this spiritual path is the door we have been seeking the whole time; the threshold is one we may have been lingering on a long time. However that encounter with a living spiritual tradition may take place, it always remains the turning point of life. It remains in consciousness as a kind of timeless moment in personal history, not just another event among others, but a central point, wherever it occurred, whether at the beginning or at the end. It becomes the pivotal point around which all other events gradually constellate. By the grace of the Spirit working within the raw experience and the questioning of experience we find the spiritual path. We have the sense at long last of really beginning. And indeed it is a new beginning.

We have begun to discover that other dimension of consciousness, spirit, which is genuinely infinite. It is not merely endless because of reflecting itself the whole time. It is authentically eternal because it is the dimension of God. There is never boredom, depression, or cynicism when we are pivoted in this dynamic dimension. Instead, we begin to discover not only the truth-relations between the world of the senses and the world of mind but the universe of the heart, the spiritual world where experience and knowledge are brought together. Here, to know something is to experience it, and to experience it is to know it with absolute truth – *love*.

Here too we face a challenge that is not the finitude of the endless or the sadness of the finite, but an opportunity, soon sensed to be an invitation to fullness of experience and to complete understanding. The challenge is not to try to experience everything or to know everything. It is to love everything. There is a great human dilemma, until we are firmly rooted in the heart, and knowledge and experience are integrated, and *we* are finally unified. It is the dilemma of the tension, even at times the violent conflict, between the general and the particular, between me and the world, between me and other people. Until we are rooted in the moving pilgrimage, until we have fully stepped through the door which begins the spiritual journey, then the universal will always seem threatening. The particular will respond as if it is going to be swamped or overwhelmed. But once we have stepped across the threshold of the survival instinct – that is the work of faith expressed in commitment and daily perseverance to the spiritual path – then the universal and the particular are no longer felt to be a threat or tension, but are united in a relationship of love.

If we see only the universal we enter abstraction. We become estranged from our own ordinariness and the ordinariness of the world. The world of particularity, ordinary daily events, our fluctuating emotional life, and day-to-day relationships, seem to be too much, too irritating, too distracting. They seem to be 'getting in the way'. If we see only the particular, though, we become coarsened. Lost in multiplicity, we fail to see the pattern and the design that gives meaning. We need to see both, not separately, but in the unifying vision of the 'sound eye' that Jesus talks about – with the healthy, unified eye of the heart. The whole purpose of meditation is to open this single eye by bringing the mind, and the experience it works on, into the heart: to become one. The way is the simple way of commitment. We commit ourselves to something as simple as the mantra which is the supreme unifier, the single path, the great harmoniser. To commit ourselves to the mantra means to commit ourselves to a vision of life as a single reality experienced, known and loved as a journey into God. To commit ourselves to the mantra means to commit ourselves to the discipline of faith and to love that discipline selflessly. To commit ourselves to the mantra within the priceless gift of faith we have received, will lead to a more enlightened seeing of Jesus and a more complete union with him.

We can only see the Risen Jesus with the vision of faith

which is the property of the eye of the heart. We can only see Jesus when we love him. He sees us, each and all of us, only because he loves us. The great hope we have on this journey, that has already brought us so far and will take us all the way, is that his love is unifying our mind and heart. It is bringing knowledge and experience together. The sign of this change taking place in the person we are is that gradually, step by step, we are learning to love, to love every particular with the universal love of God.

> Anyone who loves me will heed what I say. Then my Father will love him and will come to him and make our dwelling with him. But he who does not love me does not heed what I say. And the word you hear is not mine. It is the word of the Father who sent me. I have told you all this while I am still here with you, but your advocate, the Holy Spirit, whom the Father will send in my name will teach you everything. If you love me you will obey my commands.   (John 14:15–23, *paraphrased*)

When Jesus asks us to love him he is inviting us to see him. We see him with that power of vision that is the power of love and which he gives us through the Holy Spirit. The great mystery of the journey is that the beginning, the middle and the end are all known to God because they are all unified in his love.

The Sun

If you felt that you did not get everything done today that you had intended, do not worry. It is maybe because it was the shortest day of the year.* Even as city-dwellers the shortest day of the year makes us think of the sun and of the ubiquitous symbol of the sun in human thought. Perhaps the earliest symbol by which human beings expressed their consciousness of God, it is the most universal religious symbol that Man has conceived. It is such a primary symbol, an archetype, because the sun is the evident source of life on earth and without it the planet would abruptly cease to be. It is the most simple and therefore one of the most perfect symbols of God.

When we are simple we are humble, and then we know and acknowledge that we do not create ourselves because we are not the source of our own being. This is a very obvious idea, at least for religious people, but one that we rapidly forget and rarely act on. The structure of human reality is built on the fact or revelation that we have an origin beyond ourselves and therefore our beginning is mystery. Humanity is mystery, even to itself. And the human mystery suggests that we share something in common with the mystery that is the divine beyond. It is not only other people, Nature or God that are mysterious to us. We are a mystery for ourselves. We lose this simplicity very rapidly under certain pressures, and when we do we also lose the humility of acknowledging what we cannot understand. We become proud as we become subjected to the illusion that we are not a mystery with a transcendent origin, but a problem of the here and now. If so, there must be a combination lock and if you find the right combination you spring the lock and solve the mystery. We have today largely ceased to be spiritual in relation to ourselves, we have become crudely technological.

* 21 December 1987.

6

Today what is mysterious is usually surrendered to the occult, the psychic or to the superstitions of psycho-astrology.

Everyone is conditioned, in a non-religious society, to pride of this kind and it is pride that makes for activists. Thinking that we will solve the problem, we find there are more and more problems generated by our own complexity. It seems natural that we will solve the problems by doing more, making more, talking or studying more. Complexity, in economic or in psychological terms, generates activity. We can easily find ourselves running around in meaningless circles, trying to find meaning. But the more we suspect the hopelessness of it, the more we have to run to evade it. Eventually pride has a fall and then, through the hurt in that fall, there is a great opportunity to come to our senses. It is probably after that fall that we begin to meditate, or at least to begin seriously to listen to the teaching of a tradition that connects us without interruption to the source of consciousness where humanity is simple, humble, and in the truth. To enter upon this path of meditation is to find a way that is in direct contact with the awakening of human consciousness. But this is not a going back. We have to go forward after a fall. There is no point in going back to where you were before you fell. So, to begin to meditate means to learn from your mistakes.

Meditation is a way towards a higher and more mature simplicity, not a regression to infantilism or pre-conscious security. It leads, also, towards a humility that brings us to true self-knowledge and self-acceptance and so to the transforming knowledge of God. In meditation we are not doing, talking or making anything happen; we are not solving problems of identity; we are not trying to solve the big or small problems of life. We have plenty of other opportunities during the day to solve problems and to think about agenda. It would be most foolish to waste those precious times of meditation, thinking about ourselves, or dissecting our only too familiar problems.

Rather than doing, we are being. And by being, the way is found into the mystery. So, during the times of meditation, prepare to leave all thought behind. It is not a time for thinking at all. We are not thinking about today, yesterday or tomorrow. We are not thinking about ourselves, which is probably what we are all thinking about now. Nor is meditation a time for thinking about God. We leave all thought behind, because thought is an activity of the mind. There are multiple forms of mental activity and none are exempted: thoughts about what we should do or what we would like. Have we sent cards to everyone? Shall I take the car to the carwash? Have I got a big enough turkey? Even the distractions that we might think are rather more edifying, more abstract or religious thoughts, speculative ideas of God, of the Spirit, of my soul, of what Christmas means spiritually. All thoughts must be left behind because the mind is learning to be still – not doing. That does not mean that the mind goes to sleep. Being so cerebral, it seems to us that if we are not thinking, we are just about to go off to sleep where mental activity is automatic, dream rather than thought. What is there to do if the mind is neither thinking nor dreaming? The question troubles us because we have forgotten another state of consciousness, called prayer.

When we meditate we are not 'doing' anything with the body. Movement is an activity of the body. In meditation the body like the mind is being still. So when you meditate try and sit as still and as quietly as you can. Stillness of body and mind brings us to unity and this is the beginning of the journey to union. We need some way to help us to that stillness because the mind in particular is so active, so restless. We are given the mantra to help us, a single sacred word to repeat continually in the mind, in the heart, to sound it, listen to it and recite it from the beginning to the end of each meditation.

To follow this way, it is necessary to build into your life, on a daily basis, morning and evening, two half-hour periods of meditation. The best times are early morning before the day's activity and early evening, ideally after the day's activity. The sun's daily journey, apparently moving but really still, frames the human times of prayer. At sunrise and sunset we build upwards, on two pillars of prayer, the arch of our days. These two experiences of being that hold up the activity of the day are the times of interiority which transform the lives that obey them.

Every thing is energy and all energy is dynamic, part of a cosmic process of transformation. The energy of humanity is being converted into the energy of God. There is nothing that is not changing. A human being is woven into a unity of different strands or filaments of energy – physical, mental, spiritual – and we are in a constant energy flow. But all energy has a common source – the ground of being, not *a* being but Being itself, God. In God's image we are conscious energy, and consciousness makes the vital difference between us and other forms of created energy, but we retain the other kinds still woven into us. We are organic, we are animal, we are spirit. What is all this energy for? What does meditation do?

I once saw a film of a solar energy plant in some vast desert. For as far as the eye could see there were thousands and thousands of highly polished solar energy panels dead still, sitting there expectant but dull. In a moment somebody somewhere threw a switch and all together these panels gently turned – maybe only a few centimetres, but suddenly they were all facing the sun. Every one of them fully reflected the sun and the collective result was blinding.

Meditation is simply turning towards the sun, the source, towards God. It is not a passive thing to do because we are not turned. We turn. We choose to turn. The mantra is like the lever that turns consciousness from the centre, outward and inward simultaneously, so that we fully reflect the light of the Source which is both within us and all around us. In turning completely, one day, we will be fully enlightened, fully energised. It is difficult to believe that, because it is difficult to see that meditation is an activity of such power. It is so much more than just relaxation! Western people have come to understand energy only in terms of what we do, make or think, but we are beginning to recover the awareness of contemplation, prayer, as the purest form of energy in action, because it involves Being itself. Like good technocrats we ask how long will it take and how will things be different? How long depends entirely upon ourselves. It depends upon how quickly we turn fully to face the sun (how freely we commit ourselves to the simplicity of the mantra). How long depends also upon how often we turn back. It will also depend, somewhat, upon the kind of eagerness or energy level that we have to begin with, on the kind of person we are, and on what kind of fall we had before we began to turn.

One great reassurance is that, however long it takes, this is the way and it *will* happen. All our constituent powers, all personal levels of energy will be focused in unity into the one point that is pure Spirit. What will happen is that we will be fully converted energy, fully ourselves, fully alive in love, the all-creative energy. The process of creation will be completed. Of this, Jesus is the great sign. The divinised human being, it is in him we see the light of God focused fully in a single human being, as if his human nature were the lens that caught all the light of the sun in one small but intense point of light. We see his human nature returning to the light, which is his Source, throughout his life but fully in the death, resurrection and ascension of his body. Because he is fully human he is our enlightenment. His birth is the beginning of our divinisation because all human nature is unified in his single human nature. We too are part of his Body that focuses the divine light and bursts into the endless energy of love.

Meditation is simply turning towards this light, the pure direct light of God at the centre of each person. The mantra, saying it simply and faithfully throughout the meditation, turns and keeps us turned toward it.

> Here is the message we heard from him and pass on to you: that God is light, and in him there is no darkness at all . . . The real light already shines. Christ has made this true, and it is true in your own experience . . . What we shall be has not yet been disclosed, but we know that when it is disclosed we shall be like him, because we shall see him as he is.   (1 John 1:5; 2:8, 3:2).

Wisdom For All

One of the great tensions in the Western mind for the last two or three hundred years has been the perceived opposition of science and religion. In our own day there is the beginning of a perception of something these complementary sides of the mind have in common and which, therefore, transcends them both. This is wisdom, not seen as merely sage advice and common sense, but as the vision of unity in all aspects of reality. The scientific method will always be opposed to the religious instinct, and a confusion of the two achieves triteness not wisdom. But for the Christian this debate is raised to a higher level in the personification of wisdom in the person who unites all things in heaven and on earth, all things of science and of religion.

I was in a bookshop recently and explored a whole section devoted to ancient forms of wisdom and divination. There were innumerable books and boxed sets of everything that was once mysteriously esoteric: the I-ching, the Tarot, Runes, Egyptian hieroglyphics. It was an attractive supermarket of ancient wisdom at your fingertips, packaged with easy-to-understand directions that anyone could use. Looking at it those words of St Paul to the Colossians came to mind:

> He rescued us from the domain of darkness and brought us away into the kingdom of his dear Son, in whom our release is secured and our sins forgiven. He is the image of the invisible God; his is the primacy over all created things. In him everything in heaven and on earth was created, not only things visible but also the invisible orders of thrones, sovereignties, authorities and powers: the whole universe has been created through him and for him.   (Col. 1:13–16)

It would be easy to dismiss the section in that bookstore as New Age commercialism, or to feel superior to it because it so

11

openly manifests such spiritual hunger and religious rootless-ness. As most of us do not know much about these ancient wisdoms on the whole, it is easier to smirk at the foolishness of packaged wisdom and the gullibility that supports such popular esotericism.

But if we take St Paul's words about Jesus seriously then we should be able to do more than brusquely dismiss, in a superior tone, what all those pre-Christian forms of wisdom represent. They reveal something about our society, about the collective personality of the time we live in; that we are a people searching for wisdom and for a spiritual path. It may be trivialised and exploited by commercial entrepreneurs, making things into fads and fashions, but the search is genuine. We cannot create a fad unless there is at least the beginning of an interest. Those shelves also tell us something about the failure of Christianity.

Almost the only Christian books on sale were the Bible and the picture book of the television series on Jesus. We might have expected this, as most people only buy Bibles for babies or graduates and the televised Jesus is less demanding a cult figure than the Jesus of the gospels. Nevertheless it made me wonder what really has happened in the last 2000 years. It says something about the failure of the churches, with all their solemnly anguished divisions, to respond to that deep-seated need of human beings for wisdom, for truth, for spiritual knowl-edge. But it is not just a failure of modern Christians. We may be pretty inept at living the Gospel. We may believe in it insufficiently. We may be unable to live the teaching of Jesus without contradicting it by legalising it. We sound dogmatic or pious in attempting to communicate it to our contemporaries. Yet it is a failure that has characterised Christianity in every period. St Augustine and St Ambrose were always decrying the pagan practices continued by new converts. In the early Church the new Christians were told to give up their ancestral rites and practices but replied that they could not. The God of Christian-ity is fine for the next world, they said, but we have to keep in with the gods of this world until we get to the next.

That is an attitude in which we are all implicated. We all keep in with the gods of this world – just in case. The ancient forms of wisdom, such as were on sale in that bookshop, have their modern counterparts too. It is important that we should be able to see what our modern non-Christian forms of divination are. Our fascination and preoccupation with the psyche, our concern with self-understanding and self-development are contemporary forms of esoteric knowledge. We need the mediation of experts, the soft-spoken heirs of druids and shamans, to decipher the new symbolic language we have discovered in the inner universe of the mind. Psychology and therapy are forms and powers in which we put supernatural faith and hope and in which we hope to find wisdom, truth and infallible advice. And to a degree we can. It is not that these demo-esoteric powers, whether ancient or modern, do not have access to wisdom or wield real power. But it is that, for us, they are subject to Christ. All ways of wisdom are subordinate to wisdom itself. They are paths to *see* wisdom but in Christ we *experience* wisdom.

The thirst for knowledge goes deep in us. If we pursue it, it will take us to that depth where we find God. We want to know what we are like, we want to know who we are, we want to know what is going to happen tomorrow. Bernard Lonergan said that the hunger for knowledge is the human being's deepest need. But what is the knowledge that we are seeking and so hungry for? Is it just knowledge *about* something? Or is it *knowing* itself? Do we want to know about wisdom or do we want to know wisdom? Christ as wisdom personified, shows that knowledge is personal and wisdom is not an idea. It is not conceptual, not a 'hidden' knowledge. It is the knowledge of the personal God. We are here much closer to the biblical sense of the word 'knowledge' than the modern, computerised sense of 'knowledge' as 'information about'. The spiritual, biblical sense of knowing is ultimately synonymous with 'loving'. What Christ's humanity teaches is not another way of wisdom but wisdom itself, not divination but divinisation. We are caught by this teaching because it addresses our deepest need, for love. But it also teaches that that need is deeper than any insecurity which the earlier forms of wisdom sought to allay.

You do not see many cribs around at Christmas these days. In the department stores on Fifth Avenue or Oxford Street the Christmas displays are significantly composed of pre-Christian mythologies – little goblins, fairies and elves. Christianity is distinctly embarrassing in the marketplace, more so perhaps because of its association with the denial of pleasure than with its celebration of Incarnation. When, however, you do see a crib you find the Magi, the wise men of the East who had dreamed, divined and followed the star. Their methods had led them to the newborn child in the manger. You see human divination kneeling in adoration before divinity humanised: in a child. The three wise men represent the old forms of wisdom, the greatest and most developed insights that humanity owned. Kneeling before Christ they symbolise the culmination of all method in the humility of worship. For the Magi were both scientist and sorcerer. They employed the scientific and religious method without opposition, and so they could naturally fall on both knees before the reality that united and transcended all method. The life of the Child they worshipped went on to reveal that wisdom is love. That is the teaching of Jesus, esoteric only to those who cling to method, who fall only on to one knee.

'Love one another.' For those still following the old paths of wisdom that is not a bad teaching. But it seems to them a lower form of wisdom, the kind of wisdom that ordinary people would follow. But the 'deep stuff, the big stuff', the real secrets, are reserved for the elite. Happy – and secure – are those who believe that love is the highest, the deepest and the purest wisdom.

It is wisdom revealed in the supreme symbol of the newborn child, vulnerable, powerless, dependent. The old wisdom sought and still seeks the cleverest, the strongest and most powerful specimens of humanity. It worships the respectable, the useful, the influential people we like to be seen with, and who have got something to give or teach us. The old wisdom rejects or at best ignores others. But Christian wisdom prefers to seek out the rejects, the worst specimens of humanity, the failures, the unloved, the homeless, those for whom there is no room at the inn, the thirsty, the sick and the naked. We do not have to travel far to find them. They are there in our life already. Finding them we cannot but see ourselves as well as Christ in them and admit that there are ways in which we ourselves are sick, hungry and homeless.

For the Christian, meditation is not a way to esoteric knowledge. It is a way to greater love. It is not a way of speculation but of practice. What we are practising is a humble, simple, childlike work. The mantra opens the eye of wisdom in those who practise it in faith, because it opens the deepest centre to release the power of Christ. The love that enables us to love one another, the passion of Christ is the love of God who loves, not with self-interest but with reckless generosity. In loving we come to the only knowledge that counts and that is the knowledge that God is love.

Yet I do speak words of wisdom to those who are ripe for it, not a wisdom belonging to this passing age, nor to any of its governing powers, which are declining to their end; I speak God's hidden wisdom, his secret purpose framed from the very beginning to bring us to our full glory. (1 Cor. 2:6–7)

The Good and the Happy

The gap between what we think and believe and what we do and feel can be very considerable. For everyone, except the child or the saint, perhaps, such a gap exists. In the extreme we sense this gap as inauthenticity, hypocrisy or as evidence that human beings are not capable of the absolute. What often goes by the name of common sense makes the best of this and the questions that torment us in theoretical discussions are generally deflated by the problems in the family, the politics of the common room or the hopes and anxieties of love. Truth and pleasure form a marriage made in heaven but they squabble endlessly on earth.

Yet, for all of us, there is one very important, practical abstraction in the relationship between goodness and happiness. Can we be good and happy? Can we be happy if we are *not* good? Plato said that the good man would be able to do anything he wanted and yet never depart from the way of truth. That is the goal of any life that would be fully human and fully alive. But how to achieve it? I suppose most people have a tendency to see happiness and religion as being, if not exactly opposed, a long way from being good friends. Because of the association between religion and repression or restraint, most normal people, even religious people, have a healthy respect for the irreligious as well.

It is convenient, then, for us to compartmentalise our religious and spiritual selves into neat ranks facing the irreligious self which looks upon religious discipline as a conformist restriction of liberty. Religion prevents us from doing what we want to do or from being what we want to be. Religion points the way to the true and the ideal. Although this contradiction may be unconscious it is an attitude which often resists the integrating function of meditation. Our divided self makes meditation difficult because we feel in one part of ourselves that in meditation we are pursuing goodness at the expense of happiness. Perhaps this is why the whole notion of transcendence is difficult to accept. It is hard to reconcile needs and desires, spirit and flesh, interiority and externality. But meditation is the means of reconciliation and unity because it is the simplest thing there is. It is the most natural way to make daily life into a spiritual path.

The great religious saints and thinkers have at some point broken out of the attitude which forced a confrontation between happiness and goodness. They have seen the spiritual path as the way to beatitude, a word that can be translated either as happiness or blessedness. True happiness for them is not a result of restriction or repression but a fruit of fulfilment and liberation. In the Sermon on the Mount, the word *makarios* combines 'blessed' and 'happy'. Like many of the sayings of Jesus, the Beatitudes are expressions of paradox, harmonising what at an unspiritual level of awareness we perceive as mutually repellent. Happiness and poverty. Power and weakness. Success and failure.

Meditation is simply the way that we, who are *not* great saints or thinkers, also break through the constrictions of those falsifying dualities and so break into the discovery of what happiness is. With that breakthrough comes the experiential understanding that helps us to see what Plato meant by the good and the happy being in harmony, because the good man or woman intuitively follows the light in their own heart. There is no more important goal than to find a way to grow into this wholeness. It is all very well to think or dream about it, but we can be imagining it for the rest of our lives. We have to find a way to do it, a way to break through the nets of false attitudes and release the light of true happiness in our hearts. No way will be easy because those attitudes are deeply engrained. But meditation is the simplest way. It is as simple as practising the very simple discipline that is entailed. We practise it in short periods of daily stillness and silence: moments of prayer that fill life with the power of transcendence.

The transformation of duality into unity is sensed at every level of experience: psychological, mental and physical. But the point from which this process of oneing originates is not susceptible to analysis. So, in meditation itself, be everything, expect nothing. Do not worry about anything except saying the mantra. Do not worry about anything that 'should' happen or 'might' happen. The best way to approach meditation is to make up your mind that *nothing* is going to happen and that if anything does happen to ignore it and keep on saying your word.

It is the simplicity of this poverty of spirit – spiritual non-acquisitiveness – that makes it so certain. If it were complex there would always be something to argue about or suspect, but it is irreducibly simple. As we progress in meditation we become more simple. We come to understand that it is simplicity that makes it a sure way. And the further we follow the path the simpler, the more certain, it becomes. But because it becomes clearer and more certain does not mean we won't be tempted to temper its purity, to reduce our own commitment. Certainty demands more, not less faith. When you begin to meditate it is best to grasp straightaway that it is simplicity which is the power you will encounter. That is difficult to grasp because we begin as complex beings, trained to respect complexity and see progress as complication. We easily confuse simplicity with naïveté.

But daily experience and relationships teach the truth that the simpler we are the better and happier we are. When we become complex we become weak, confused and begin to wander. Simplicity however demands work. It is not easy to attain or retain. It is the struggle of the ascent of being that Plato also speaks about. The struggle to become good is one with the work of being happy. If simplicity demands work, if meditation is challenging, it is because in the state of simplicity all opposites arising from the conflicts within ourselves are resolved.

Another important attitude to have at the outset as one begins to meditate is patience. It is curious how impatient we are with regard to meditation, looking for immediate results, instant enlightenment, quick vision. Yet we are quite prepared to be patient in training for a profession. Three, five or seven years seem reasonable to accept as training for a qualification. People are even more prepared for patience when going on a diet or trying out new exercises. Psychoanalysis is built upon the premise of perseverance. We have to learn an even deeper patience and perseverance in order to meditate. But what we come to understand is that in a real sense meditation is, in itself, a *being patient*. It is being present. It is not running ahead to planning tomorrow. It is not running back doing a postmortem on yesterday. It is not about grabbing any experience, spiritually, psychologically or physically. It is not about trying to possess anything. It is far more about letting go than acquiring. And this, curiously enough, is precisely why meditation is the way to true happiness.

Unhappiness begins the moment we enter the innately complex state of desire, when we establish a division between what we are and what we want. If we are unhappy about being unhappy so much of the time, it is because we spend so much of the time preoccupied with what we want, scheming for our desires or – and this is really just an inverse variation on desire – regretting what we missed or lost or bewailing our mistakes. The great illusion that holds human beings in slavery to the unhappiness of their own desires is the fantasy that they will become happy automatically as soon as they get what they want. This assumption (as soon as one challenges it, one realises how deeply engrained it is) that happiness is getting what we want, is what we unlearn in meditation and what meditation frees us from. In our society that assumption is so deeply dyed into us that we are hardly aware of it or even able to question it. It is so much the prevailing belief that we blithely call ourselves consumers in a consumer society. Survival seems to depend upon taking what we want, and to desire something is to acquire a right to it. Here is the state of spiritual blindness, the state of unrestrained egoism, in which, thinking that we know what we are doing, we are in fact walking through life with our eyes shut. Prepared to sacrifice everything we have been sacredly given in order to get what we want, or have been induced and seduced to desire, we lose the real treasure of our own spirit and, with it, real happiness of heart. We perpetually sacrifice happiness for desire in the *samsara* of consumerism and greedy entrepreneurism. There is no end to wandering in that darkness because desire is circular. However many times we may learn that we have built upon the shifting ground of an illusion, the illusion re-forms when the tide of desire returns and we commit the same unhappy mistakes again. Christianity has traditionally emphasised this pattern with regard to sexuality, where it is certainly present. But sexuality has been heavily over-emphasised and the dangers of desire in other human activities need to be recognised more urgently.

There is a way. It is so simple and direct that we can walk unbelievingly straight past it. Meditation allows us to leave that cycle of egoism by unhooking us, little by little, from the self-centredness which has us believe the illusion that we would be happy if we could get everything we want. Meditation helps us to unlearn the patterns of behaviour based on that illusion, and therefore meditation very radically changes your life. You will change the way you live as a result of meditation because it will change the way you relate to yourself, to others, to your work. It will introduce a new spirit of love into your life. Illusions are only permanently unlearned by experiencing truth in the form of paradox. We experience truth in the paradox that the way of liberty and happiness is the way of simplicity and discipline. That is the way of meditation, the way of the mantra.

But to enter that revitalising paradox we need to learn to be undistracted. All desire, all self-centred pursuit of happiness is technically a distraction, and meditation explains this to us not as philosophy or as moral imperative but as experience. The experience is of the truth found in the centre of the human self. It is the truth that will set us free from selfishness, the truth that is happiness, the truth that Jesus has made selfless within us through his Spirit.

This Spirit teaches us that we should not pursue happiness as a goal because that would be to be self-centred and therefore unreal, because God is the centre, not ourselves. God is the goal, Truth is God and what we must pursue is the Truth. Meditation makes us truthful. Jesus called this goal the Kingdom. He told us that the Kingdom is interior, not an object of desire but a potency patient to our realising it. He shows us that if we set our mind on this goal without distraction then unimaginable fullness will come to us with a happiness greater than we could ever want. The way beyond distraction and desire is the way of the mantra, setting our mind simply and clearly on the Kingdom.

I bid you therefore put away anxious thoughts about food and drink to keep you alive, and clothes to cover your body. Surely life is more than food, the body more than clothes

. . . Why be anxious about clothes? Consider how the lilies grow in the fields; they do not work, they do not spin; and yet, I tell you, even Solomon in all his splendour was not attired like one of these . . . Set your mind on God's kingdom and his justice before everything else, and all the rest will come to you as well.   (Matt. 6:25–6, 28–9, 33)

Remaining Free

There is a story told by Solzenitsyn from the period of the Stalin terror of a political meeting in a small Russian town. A petty official of the party had come to give a talk to the local cell. It was a remarkably boring talk full of platitudes and nonsense, and everyone sat listening to it with stony faces and when he finished they all stiffly stood up and began to applaud. The applause went on and on and on and nobody dared to be the first to stop applauding because that would show a disloyal lack of enthusiasm or orthodoxy. So the heartless applause went on for a good ten minutes until the local secretary of the party decided to be brave and was the first to stop applauding and sit down. Predictably, he disappeared the following week.

It is a story that is both absurd and frightening. It reveals how easily we can lose freedom, and what that meeting testified to was the nightmare world of fear that follows the loss of freedom. The experience at the heart of meditation confronts that nightmare, usually repressed in us, and awakens us to true liberty. When you are beginning to meditate and you realise after a few weeks what kind of discipline is being asked of you, it is quite natural to ask, 'What is meditation really going to do for me? Here am I trying to meditate every day, trying to be faithful to these two periods of meditation, morning and evening and what now?' The novelty wears off after a while. You realise you are not going to get enlightened in the first two weeks. Later you realise that something deeper is happening, something deeper is being awakened. But *what* is meditation doing for me?

It is a difficult question to answer, except by the personal knowledge we have of someone who has been meditating for some time. One thing we can say that meditation will do is make us more free. We are likely to say to this at first, 'Well it's all very well to be free but will meditation give me what I want?' That is the more immediate concern: 'Will I get what I want? I can see more clearly than ever all the things I am lacking, all the things that I believe would make me complete and whole and happy. If I could just get these, then I could be free and then maybe I could be good or at least nice.' It is difficult to allow meditation to teach us that it will do more than give us what we want. It will free us from the fears that all desire creates. If we focus upon desires we immediately enter the realm of fears. We fear failure, we fear loss, we fear non-achievement, we fear not becoming or doing what we want to be or do. We are inmates of the inner *gulag* of fear, a reign of terror.

Freedom is the absence of fear and it is the true use of freedom to be your own self. We are only our self if we are not another self. That is very obvious and simple because, of course, we cannot be anyone else. We can only be the person we are. But, although it is impossible to be someone else, it is quite possible to act as if we were someone else. We act other than what we are either through rejection or through projection. If we have known or felt rejection it is likely that we have interiorised it and lost faith in that part of ourselves that was (really or delusively) rejected. A major part of human interaction involves projecting what is in us, or not in us, on to others. This delusion that we are not ourselves or are someone else is the root of most mistakes and perhaps of all suffering.

To be one's own self is as simple as it sounds, but it is more demanding than it seems. It requires the real work of withdrawing our projections and of cutting loose the fears that bind us. This work of freedom, of becoming free, is usually called 'detachment' in spiritual language. Detachment is the positive meaning of the death experience. It always comes to us one way or another whether we voluntarily accept it or resist it. Detachment always releases the taste of freedom, the exhilaration of liberty, even when it comes in the form of losing something that is precious to us, something good. Often we do not see the freedom it gives because we do not want freedom. We see only what we want. We want what we want. We do not want freedom. Therefore, we respond to detachment by finding something else to cling to as quickly as possible after the loss occurs. This explains the lifeless unfreedom that

23

religious life or the spiritual path can become after the most promising and vital beginnings in joyful renunciation. It explains why we need more than one exposure to the truth to become free.

If we want to be free it must be the only thing worth wanting because it is the only thing that cannot be taken away from us. Freedom so often comes to people when it would seem that they are most unfree, most committed, most caught up or involved. But we need a way to continue to let go; not just to let go once, but to continue letting go and to make sure that we do not start clinging as soon as we begin to fear the dizziness of the peaks of freedom. That is why we need a way, a practice. That is why we need to meditate.

Above all, to be free, to be our self, we must detach ourselves from the crowd. The crowd is an animal begotten by hidden fears. It is full of aggression, held together by fears of what is not inside it. It becomes violent because of fear. The crowd always turns upon the free person because of its own fear of freedom. The problem for the free, however, is that this does not mean that we must assert our individuality to remain free. In fact crowds are first formed into non-being by the super-egoists who assert their individuality at any cost, at the cost of those around them. The free are able to be themselves in communion and do not need an impersonal collectivity to assert their otherwise insecure or envious ego.

Leaving the crowd is always the first step on the spiritual path. It is the first and solitary step in being our self and it is much more of an interior process than we may think. What often seems to be being our selves is merely an assertion of the ego, trying to be different, trying to be special, trying to be separate, trying to be the winner. But leaving the crowd is a detachment from the ego and a discovery, not of isolation, but of involvement and relationship with others. The real crowd we must escape from; the real prison is within ourselves. We do not see it very often. Often the bars we rail at for keeping others in are actually surrounding us, keeping others out. We think the crowd is outside ourselves and so blame something outside of ourselves for any lack of freedom we feel. But the crowd that deprives us of freedom is interiorised. We have first of all to throw the spotlight on it, even though that may be uncomfortable and unpleasant. Coming to know ourselves is

no pleasant matter. But we have to be able to see the cause of
the unfreedom and we do see it in a very simple way by sitting
in stillness of body and mind.

By sitting still for half an hour each morning and each evening you will meet the crowd. And in meeting it you will free
yourself from it. The inner crowd is made up of all the splintered selves that the ego keeps producing; all the voices that
clamour competitively for recognition, for self-assertion, for
domination; all those wounded and broken parts of ourselves,
the little bits of our experience, the dangling ends of unfinished
stories; the desires and fears with their unrestrained voices
crying for the unattainable. The crowd is always desperate
because it feels that what it longs for is not there – whereas its
desires can only be attained when it becomes whole, becomes
a single self. The noise of the crowd in us is the flow of mental
distraction. When you meditate you will experience that crowd
and the disharmony of the splintered self in the form of distractions. There is not one of us who does not experience some
degree of distraction when we meditate. But the way of meditation is not to be mapped by anything so superficial as our
distractions. It is to be read by the scale of life itself. We will
know we are free when we are free to say the mantra in all
simplicity and love. The way to freedom through the crowd of
distractions is to say the mantra.

The mantra leads to freedom because it leads to the self. As
it pursues its wonderfully direct and accurate course, the mantra
will integrate, unite, harmonise, all the splintered selves and it
will make one self, our true self. Jesus said that truth sets us
free. Truth is not just an idea and no amount of thinking will
make us free. Truth is a reality-experience of the whole person.
Prayer is the pure experience of truth. It is into prayer that we
enter as we meditate. We enter, in the Christian vision, into the
prayer of Christ, into his experience, ultimate and complete, of
the truth that God is truth. We can only really experience the
truth of God by entering it, by being one with it in the solitude
which we must abandon the crowd to find. If our self is one
with God it is because of its union with Christ. The fact that
this is possible for us is the hope of a reality that changes our
life once we have seen it. We see it if we can simply meditate,
if we can simply be ourselves. We do not have to look for it

to happen because it will be happening within us, not outside us.

The Pharisees asked him, 'When will the kingdom of God come?' He said, 'You cannot tell by observation when the kingdom of God comes. There will be no saying, 'Look, here it is!' or 'there it is!'; for in fact the kingdom of God is within you.   (Luke 17:20-1)

The Joy of Wanting Nothing

If there is one thing we can be sure about the future it is that we will always be wanting something. Whatever happens, whatever we get, we will always be wanting something. Human beings are always looking for something or aspiring to something. It is a characteristic of human nature to be nearly always aware of a lack, of a need, or of something missing. Even at times of great happiness and satisfaction that awareness of something missing is never far away. All the great religious traditions take account of this state of desire that we live in. They do not try to deny it. They accept that human beings are in the state of desire, and most of them see the connection between desire and other human characteristics, such as anxiety, suffering or sin. The Buddha's way of liberation, for example, taught the escape from suffering through the elimination of desire. Get rid of desire and the desiring ego, and there will be no more suffering. He taught the way of mindful detachment. The teaching of Jesus no less recognises that when we are over-concerned with our material needs or status we will be in a condition of anxiety and disharmony in relation to others and to God. His solution was correspondingly simple – not to try to renounce our needs one by one, because that would be an endless task, but rather to go to the root of desire and to transcend that, to leave self behind. 'Set your mind on the kingdom before everything else, and everything else will come to you as well.'

It is not easy to follow such a simple, radical teaching, but if we can even approach the experience of its truth we will discover its possibility. If we can take our attention off our needs even for a short period we will discover the extraordinary transforming effect that a redirected consciousness has on us, as we live our daily lives, cope with emotions and anxieties of every kind. This is precisely what meditation does. It does so

27

in an undramatic way. But the revolution-conversion it works is the drama of redemption from suffering to joy. Meditation reveals our role in the story not as anything remote or esoteric, or as something that only the great sages or mystics can achieve, but in a way that is as human as desire itself.

It is as human to transcend desire as to be controlled by it. That is why in every major religious tradition you find the way of meditation. You find it as a way that builds periods of desirelessness into the ordinary textures and rhythms of daily life. These short periods where we work at a purely spiritual exercise release us into an experience of freedom and of the joy that accompanies freedom. The times of meditation are times for being, not for wanting. They are times in which we take the wanting out of being and, as a result, experience pure being and the bliss that having nothing but being generates. Those two times of daily meditation a day become times of spiritual work and times of powerful re-creation. As times of renewal and refreshment the effect of those short periods of desirelessness overflow into daily life. You are not merely recharging your batteries; you are making contact with an inexhaustible source of energy, the energy of divine being. As we make contact with it, it flows into every corner of life with all its unlimited power. The contact with the ground of being is why those two simple and ordinary half-hours of meditation each day have such a transforming effect upon our lives. As they are times of being not for wanting, do not even want any spiritual experience. Do not want anything to happen. Do not want God. Do not want the Spirit. Do not want not to want.

The fulfilment that flows from that simple experience of being is greater than anything we can want. Reality is always surprising and unpredictable. That is why it is important to be clear about the way in which we meditate and then, having become clear about it, which is not very difficult as it is quite straightforward, to stay with it. To meditate you enter a new realm of spiritual discipline. Two periods a day may seem a major commitment to make at the beginning. The sooner you can make that commitment, however, the sooner you will find that you are on the path for which twenty-four hours a day would not be disproportionate! But it may take some time to build that discipline regularly into your life. However long it takes, it will teach you patience and commitment. You undertake a very simple and immediate discipline in stillness. Not scratching your nose will be a small step beyond desire. The stillness of your body becomes a way into a stillness of mind in which the movement of desire resolves into joy. Do not think about the meaning of the mantra because that would be setting the mind in more motion, and meditation is not a way of thought.

When we start thinking we are only one step away from wanting. Let the thoughts come; but let them go, and stay with the mantra, saying it, listening to it and coming back to it continuously. Giving your attention to the mantra takes the mind off all the wanting, all the needs and all the problems and complexities that needs create. It is turning our consciousness directly away from the state of egoism. The mind will keep slipping back to its needs, to an analysis of what is lacking, to a searching-out of more things to want. The mind will keep slipping back into plans for the future, trying to seek the solution to our latest needs. But the mantra reverses that process of constant wanting as we keep coming back to it. Then meditation teaches us through the mantra, a great truth, that if we are truly seeking we will find.

Most of the time we are not really clear what we are seeking or what we desire. We are inconstant and confused about the objects of our quest. There always seems to be a need deeper than the one we have just satisfied. We have, of course, certain images of what we want. But even if we gain these we experience only a temporary relief from the ache of desiring. We become serious seekers, truly spiritual, fully human, only when we have really accepted the truth that what we are seeking is not this or that thing, person or experience, but wholeness in itself and for itself. We are not seeking wholeness because it will be a means to gaining something else we want. We are seeking a wholeness that has no need to want. We begin to meditate because we have begun to glimpse the truth that this wholeness is already within us, within our grasp. Except we cannot grasp it. We cannot possess it. But we can release it. And meditation is a releasing of this wholeness already present within us. In poverty we glimpse that truth, and even desire itself teaches it to us if we are teachable. But we become clearer about its presence within us as we go on meditating day by day, with a clarity that grows from the centre outwards and that purifies everything that we do and are.

As we become conscious of it, it expands beyond consciousness. It is released, it becomes realised. It is the unpossessable gift waiting to be received, totally simple and quite unconditional. We do not have to earn it, we do not even have to be worthy of it. We simply have to be ready to receive it and accept it. The Gospel calls this wholeness 'happiness' or 'blessedness'. The joy of the Holy Spirit characterises its realisation and this happens when the timing is right, when we are ready. All we have to do is to be alert and awake and then the conditions for realising the gift are there. The Spirit, that is the wholeness within us, is like a buried treasure. The digging may be hard, but as we dig we come across little rivulets of joy. Sometimes they will flow for a while and then disappear and we must continue digging. We must continue saying the mantra, no matter what we feel. Do not judge your meditation as good or bad. If we keep saying the mantra, we will surely strike the mainstream and, when we do so, it will flow without ceasing. Life as a stream is the image Jesus used to describe the interiority of the kingdom in which there is too much joy to allow any space for desire.

> Jesus stood and cried aloud, 'If anyone is thirsty let him come to me; whoever believes in me, let him drink.' As Scripture says, 'Streams of living water shall flow out from within him.' He was speaking of the Spirit which believers in him would later receive.   (John 7:37–9)

The Power of Attention

John Main, in *Word into Silence*, once quoted another monk, Pope Saint Gregory the Great. Gregory was writing about St Benedict's sanctity as a portrayal of the real meaning of interiority. 'He dwelt within himself always in the presence of his Creator and never allowing his eyes to gaze on distractions.' Father John comments that this description 'tells us that, in Gregory's view, Benedict had realised a wholeness and harmony that had dispelled all false ideas, all illusions about himself, illusions which are necessarily outside of ourselves'. The monastic Fathers were always lucid and simple in understanding that the principal purpose of the monastic life is to come to an unbroken awareness of the presence of God, to continuous prayer. St Augustine, writing not only for monks but for all Christians, said that the whole purpose of life and of every Christian exercise is the permanent opening of the 'eye of the heart'. The opening of the spiritual eye is a way of expressing undifferentiated and unbroken consciousness, that pure consciousness which is the state of unceasing prayer. When the eye of the heart is truly opened, it never blinks; it never closes again.

Here is the aim of the Christian life, because it is, for each of us personally, the invitation that we have been privileged to receive in the call of Jesus to be his disciples. There has always been a great danger, but one that exists especially for us today in our self-conscious and narcissistic society, of mistaking introversion, self-fixation, self-analysis, for true interiority. The great prevalence of psychological woundedness and social alienation exacerbates this danger while calling for gentle tact and compassion in dealing with it. The test of true interiority is revealed in those words of St Gregory. 'He dwelt within himself always in the presence of his Creator and never allowing his eyes to gaze on distractions.' To be truly interior is the complete opposite of being introverted. In the awareness of the indwelling presence our consciousness is turned around, con-verted, so that we are no longer, as we have habitually been doing, looking at ourselves, anticipating or remembering feelings, reactions, desires, ideas or daydreams. But we are turning towards something else. And that is always a problem for us.

It would be easier, we think, to turn away from introspection if we knew what we were turning towards. If we only had a fixed object to look at. If only God could be represented by an image. But the true God can never be an image. Images of God are gods. To make an image of God is merely to end up looking at a refurbished image of ourselves. To be truly interior, to open the eye of the heart, means to be living within the imageless vision that is faith, and that is the vision that permits us to 'see God'. In faith attention is controlled by a new Spirit, no longer the spirits of materialism, self-seeking and self-preservation, but the ethos of faith which is by its nature dispossessive. It is always letting go and continuously renouncing the rewards of renunciation, which are very great and so all the more necessary to be returned. There is no more crucial challenge than entering the experience of remaining other-centred. It is the ecstatic and continuous state of dispossession. We can glimpse it simply by calling to mind those moments or phases in life where we experienced the highest degree of peace, fulfilment and joy and recognise that those were times, not when we possessed anything, but when we lost ourselves in something or someone. The passport into the kingdom requires the stamp of poverty.

Our attention is turned away from the multifarious workings of our consciousness when it is turned towards and into the creative centre which is the presence of God. Times of meditation are so vital to a holy and wholesome life because they are times when we give ourselves unreservedly to the primary goal of the Christian life, not moral rectitude but spiritual transformation. By the discipline of daily meditation we find that our attentiveness is becoming perceptibly more other-centred in the time-space between the periods of regular practice. This goal of mindfulness at first requires a rather disciplined resolve to limit and eventually to eschew all distraction – and anything, even the most religious things can be idolised into distractions. But, with time, the effort to be truly interior becomes less artificial, less self-conscious and becomes a natural and good 'habit' of consciousness, the authenticity of which is attested by liberty and joyfulness. The spiritual tradition insists everywhere on moderation as the discipline that prevents us falling into either of the self-destructive states of fanaticism or mediocrity. Moderation is the perennial narrow path. It is daily and ordinary.

To be attentive at all, whether in meditation or in ordinary life, to the presence of God as the primal parental unity we call Creator, we need to become attentive to Christ. But that does not mean staring at an image of him, or conducting an imaginary conversation with him. It means entering into the attentiveness of Christ himself. Contemplation is not *looking at* or *being looked at*. It is a state of unified consciousness in which the identities of self and other, subject and object are – joyfully not terribly – interchangeable. The supreme human condition of interchangeability with God is the prayer of Christ in us, his Spirit rising in us. His Spirit open to the Father, loving the Father and caught up out of himself in the reciprocal love of the Holy Spirit, this is his journey and ours to the Father who is his and ours. This is the Spirit we have received. This is the prayer of Christ and this is our prayer.

There is a very simple way to understand how the prayer of Jesus becomes our prayer. Think how natural it is when you go into a room where someone is looking up intently at the ceiling, to follow the line of their attention and to seek what has so absorbed them. Pure attention is the most powerful energy of which consciousness is capable. And it is the most communicable. Trusting the power of that single-minded purity is what we do when we pray. We give our attention to Christ and gradually our attention is empowered by his and is turned, within his consciousness, to the Father. This is the trinitarian basis of meditation, the pure attention of Jesus in the Spirit, towards the Father. This too is the true interiority of the Christian. Prayer is therefore what makes any action Christian, any ministry, service, vocation, or menial task truly Christian. It does not carry Christ-consciousness because of talking about it, making denominational signs by wearing something distinctive, or using a specifically religious kind of language or by dropping leaflets around. What makes action essentially Christian is that, deep within our own spirit, our attention is held

33

within Christ, towards the Father. This is why, as experience proves, true interiority is the basis of heart-felt charity. In the practical terms by which the daily discipline instructs us we discover, by persevering on the way of meditation, that we become more loving, more compassionate, more generous. We do so despite ourselves, despite apparent failures and despite our only too self-evident egoism and disappointing reoccurrences of egoism. Despite it all, the pull, the attentive call of the prayer of Christ, draws us into itself.

And yet learning to be other-centred is a discipline, it is discipleship and it means an ascesis. There is nothing more difficult than to learn to take the attention off ourselves. And, for us today, there is an even greater challenge to face, because it seems almost sacrilegious to take our attention off ourselves, so much do we equate growth, fulfilment and development with self-analysis and the conscious up-building of a positive self-image. Indeed we need to love ourselves, to be healed through confession, forgiveness and communion. Christian faith affirms this in the revelation of our origin and sustained being in unconditional love, in Jesus as the supreme and universal Healer and Therapist of the human soul.

But the wisdom of Jesus is absolutely simple and uncompromising in pointing the way to the wholeness of the Kingdom: we must leave our self behind. In doing so we do gain it a hundredfold because we find ourselves in everything around us, in every person, in every situation, in each successive moment. We see our self in Christ and God in Christ in everyone and everything. Maybe this will unfold vaguely at first but clarity of vision is growing. The importance of the mantra is absolute if we are committed to total simplicity. It is the mantra which allows us to keep the attention pure and directed Godward in Christ.

The mantra highlights the importance, too, of community because in becoming attentive to others, their real presence, the loving presence of Christ in others, a community is created that is turned with collective attentiveness – the prayer of the church – towards Christ. This corporate prayer of the Body is vital for us not only as a help but as a necessary structure of spiritual reality. We are all too prone to let our attention wander, to drift back into self-consciousness, self-infatuation and, when attention does drift in this false current, we soon re-enter the state of distraction. There is then a simple truth to discover. When attention is in God, with the vision of faith, everything reveals God to us. When our attention is on ourselves, in the image-blindness of the ego, everything is a distraction from God.

It seems a demanding challenge to place our attention always in that vision of faith, until we realise that that is precisely what we have been created for. In it we find our selves because we fulfil our meaning for God and for creation.

The Now of Loving

I did not really understand what meditation is about until I saw the importance of meditating every day of my life. As long as you think you can do just enough meditation to get by or enough to achieve something, you have not really begun to meditate. When you realise that you have started a journey that will last until the end of your life, you have begun to learn. That moment of recognition and assent we call commitment. It is well described as a moment of grace and understanding, because in it we experience our deepest meaning and the importance of prayer for being fully alive. We meditate, not so much to know why we are alive, but to live differently, to live more fully. As soon as we have glimpsed that live connection between meditation and life we know that meditation is coterminous with life; it is parallel with our life, and like life it is rooted in the earth with its branches in heaven. As soon as we sense that, we realise that we are learning something, that life itself can be more fully understood as a learning, as an awakening, as a discovery.

Meditation itself is a learning experience, literally a 'discipline'. Only discipline will teach us truth, and only practice will bring us to awakening. The discipline of meditation is a school. It is a school of love, and the human growth, which is the learning-process, is growth in the true discipleship of love. It teaches us what we need to know, to see with the heart, to grasp at the centre, to embrace with every fibre of our being. It teaches us what we have to know in order to fulfil the essential destiny that each human being has, to be oneself for eternity. Human destiny is for eternal living. It is easy to settle for temporary living, for less than eternal life, because we grasp the finite with less of ourselves than we are grasped by the infinite. Most of us begin to meditate at the point where we have partially settled for finite life. Yet we have also begun to realise that this was a mistake. It is easy to settle for finite life because it is a life lived within protective barriers. It seems safe and secure. In fact, it is not so easy. The most challenging option of all is to live eternally, to respond to the ultimate truth about existence, identity and death. It exceeds the power of imagination to realise that we are made for eternity, which means not only life in the world to come, but life lived fully now. And being fully alive demands everything we are at every moment. Not surprisingly, we scale down the wonder of this and construct those protective barriers of fame, power and ambition. Yet life is stronger than our fears of eternity and if we are to live at all we must live eternally, we must live fully.

Living eternally means living wholly in the present moment. Eternity is the perpetual *now*, and as we learn to live eternally in the present moment we learn the truth about love which is also entirely present. To love is to be fully present to and for the other with an intensity and unity that transcends the ravages of time. It is easy to settle for illusion about love. Romance imagines love in the past or future. What it calls love is in fact a dream of love. We have begun to meditate, to learn in the school of love, after having made the mistake of confusing the eternal and the finite, having called illusion reality, having called possessiveness love. But living eternally, in the present moment, teaches us that we erred because we did not know what love really was or from where it springs.

How do we learn that? We learn it by being loved eternally, fully. Such love continually de-objectifies the object of love. As we learn to be loved fully it becomes increasingly difficult for us to possess or to control. Because not only does love de-objectify the beloved, it also does something to the lover. It leads the lover into self-transcendence. That is the strangeness of love, the unfamiliarity of it, the alchemy of it. The object of love ceases to be an object while the lover transcends himself. This process seems to lead to the annihilation of both lover and beloved. It seems to lead to the loss of identity. If it is all letting go, if it is all transcendence, what is there to hang on to? Who *is* there? This is the challenge of knowing eternal life, to take the risk of annihilation.

Coming to fullness of being means arriving at our real identity, at the point where our name is radiant. But we come to it through what seems so like annihilation, such a strong process of un-naming, that it can best be described as death. It is the ending of one incomplete identity and the beginning of another. Of course, death is not the end. And once we have begun to love and be loved eternally, to live eternally, we realise that death is very commonplace. It happens over and over again. It is simply and always the next step. What remains the same in this recurrent loss of identity is the essential being, the essential identity of the self. What we are seems to come to an end but who we are rises again. I think we experience this in meditation in the apparent annihilation, the apparent nothingness of it, with nothing to think about, nothing to imagine, when God and the self are no longer identifiable. It is an experience of dying into fuller life.

But love is not concerned by death, and this is why the lover can smile all the way through the tears of death. Love does not seek the destruction of identity, either in the lover or the beloved. Jealousy does that, because it is the reversal and negation of love. But love is prepared to go through death in order to achieve an even higher degree of identity, the final identity being in union. St Augustine said, 'If I love you, I want you to be,' and that desire for the other to be simply and fully his or her own self is the essence of love. It is the essence of God's creative love. That God wants us to *be* is the reason for our own existence.

The parables that Jesus told about the lost sheep and the prodigal son tell of this secret of God's love for us. In those stories we see a God who is totally, eternally concerned with the identity of the beloved. God is so wholly concerned with unique identity that it defies number. He is as concerned about one sheep as about ninety-nine. He is as concerned about the prodigal son as the one who stayed at home. This is a love that finite love cannot understand and, in fact, finite love may be angered by it, because such total love seems to threaten our identity. It is a love that does not believe in mathematics, logic or protective barriers. The love of God – total, eternal – transcends number, jealousy and fear. It gives an identity that does not need any barriers to protect it. It bestows and affirms identity that does not depend upon our remaining individuals. It creates an identity that empowers us to enter into the highest identity of union where we are more than individuals, where we are undivided. It is important to learn of this eternal love, because if we forget it we soon become limited to finite loving. That means that we may soon cease to love and if we cease loving we become unloving and, in the end, inhuman. If we love only finitely then we will end up eliminating or exterminating what we find unlovable and our own century shows us how possible that horror can be. Only eternal loving can want every one to *be*.

Meditation, like the Gospel, teaches us that we are divinised by the eternal love of Jesus. In moving from finite love to eternal love, along a single spectrum of humanity, we become fully human by entering divine life. Humanity is divinised by the eternal love of God that we encounter in Jesus. That encounter is prayer. We find out then what love is and it is not at all what we thought. We discover it to be infinitely beyond the power of mind to understand or express, and infinitely beyond the power of emotion to register. But we find it to be present and real within us. We can only know it by accepting it unconditionally. We can only have eternal life if we are prepared to lose ourselves and that is what we do in the simple, loving, saying of the mantra. The love within us divinises because it makes us capable of loving eternally, like God. Or perhaps not like God, but certainly *with* God, *in* God. As we learn that, we discover the joy and the wonderful strangeness of living in the divine consciousness as a state of continual non-possession, continual giving and self-transcendence. It is no less a state in which our being and the being of the other are constantly identified, named and affirmed. The root of this is in the love that flows between the Father, the Son, and the Spirit, the unity of three that transcends number and finds similitude in the other.

> May they all be one: as thou, Father, art in me, and I in thee, so also may they be in us; that the world may believe that thou didst send me. The glory which thou gavest me I have given to them, that they may be one, as we are one; I in them and thou in me, may they be perfectly one. (John 17:20–3)

The Race Where All Win

I was once staying with a young family who had a little girl. She had just started at kindergarten and came in one evening very excited, waving a little piece of paper. She had just been awarded the certificate for being the 'best pupil of the week'. She was very excited about this and insisted that the certificate be put up on the fridge for everyone to see. You could not help but share in her thrill of excitement and pure pleasure. But, at the same time, you could not help wondering if the competitive impulse had not been stimulated a little too early. What would happen next week when some other child became the best pupil. Would that engender unnecessary feelings of jealousy, anger or a sense of failure?

It is inevitable that competitiveness will be present in human relationships and in all societies. Wherever there is an ego there is competition, even if it is to excel our own 'personal best'. There is the inevitable desire to excel, but it applies to more than our own performance or love of the work we are doing. In egoism there is the desire to exceed and surpass the performance of others, to be always in front, to be Number One. Possibly this is because, in the strange logic of the ego, we feel that we are safest there. In one form or another, this is innate in human nature. It can even be a dominant urge that affects every part of our life, intellectual, emotional, social. It is *the* dominant urge as long as we are centred in the ego and until we begin the process of transcending the ego, which is what the New Testament and Jesus call 'leaving self behind'.

In the vision of the spiritual tradition egoism is only one stage of development. It is necessary, it is inevitable, but it is only a transitional stage. We are not meant to be, nor need we be, fixed at that stage of development. Like all stages in growth, it needs to be transcended in the right kind of way, not violently or cruelly. It needs to be transcended in a way that encourages the natural process of growth that is continually going on in us – the unfolding life of our personhood – so that, when it is transcended, it can be reintegrated and permit the next stage to appear. It is possible to get stuck at any stage of the journey, to have development arrested. And here is another way of understanding sin. It does not make sense to talk of unconscious or involuntary sin. There is no sin without freedom. Yet as we – and St Paul – know from experience, our freedom is often constrained by natural forces that seem to 'make' us choose what we would rather not. The tendency to regression, to avoid the challenge of transcendence and the risk of growth, is a strong one. We can easily choose – often by omission or passivity – to let this tendency prevail. To choose not to grow is sin. The longer we remain in a state of developmental arrest, the more energy, time and faith is needed to pull us out of it and take us forward. That is why it is so important to hear the urgency of the spiritual tradition, that tells us that *now, today,* is the day of liberation.

Our society and most of its values encourage us to remain arrested at the stage of the ego. The problems that result from this are momentous. The psychological disorders of our time are endemic. Freud and other founders of psychology even at the end of the last century remarked on the alarming increase in nervous disorders. I was talking to a psychiatrist recently about this and he said that the contemporary increase was an insoluble problem. Therapy is very time-consuming and very expensive and not everyone can afford either the time or the money. So what, I asked, in the long run, and for everyone, is the answer? His solution was that therapy should begin in the classroom, with children. But it seemed to me that that was really increasing the treatment for the disease, not curing it. His only suggestion showed, I thought, how far we have lost the wisdom, which is always a practical wisdom, of our spiritual tradition. This tells us that healing *is* growth. We can naturally and therapeutically progress from one stage to another, simply by getting more deeply in touch with the spirit of life, the goodness and love of life inherent in us. We grow only if we can stay in touch with our own centre. The widespread discovery of the tradition of meditation in our time is a real sign of hope, a regenerative thrust towards health and wholeness. We can begin to meditate at any stage of our journey. Children can meditate, people can start to meditate in the last days of their life. You can begin whether you are in a natural or an arrested stage of development.

To begin, it is usually only necessary to have simple advice, personal encouragement and openness to the Spirit's guidance. Before long you find yourself, in one form or another, in the community or Body which the spiritual journey creates and which faith gives us the vision to perceive. But for some there will also be the need to have specialised help – analysis or therapy – in order to bring them to that self-knowledge which reveals self-transcendence as the basic law of growth and healing. In either case, it is only necessary to begin and the sooner one begins, the better.

Meditation is a response to that word of the tradition which tells us that *now* is the time. *Today* is the time. Anyone can begin to meditate now. Meditation is not an escape from the problems of growth in any life. It is a direct way of confronting them at root in ourselves, not in talk or theory, but in silence and personal experience. Meditation is practical wisdom, something we do, not something to think about. It is a practical way to move gently, naturally and in the right way and speed beyond egoism.

One of the signs of this rightness is that there is nothing at all competitive about meditation. Meditation is not a race. We are not trying to get anywhere before anyone else. We cannot get there before ourselves. You cannot meditate hurriedly. You set a fixed time to meditate, each morning and evening. You stick to that time regularly. You are not seeking the first place, because by beginning at all you are implicitly accepting that Christ has already won. He came in a long way ahead of us. But he has won for us, not triumphed over us. The ego's jealousy of Christ is ultimately defeated by its own absurdity, because Christ longs to share his victory with us, as equals.

Who is there to compete with? You are simply allowing yourself to be, to be yourself, to be where you are and who you are. That is why stillness is such an important element to meditation. Stillness of mind and stillness of body preclude competition or self-assertion. In the two periods of meditation each day, the first purpose is to be still. First of all, physically still. That is an important and difficult discipline to learn, to sit physically still. But secondly to be still in mind, by the very simple way of the mantra. The repetition of a single word or phrase leads to stillness and stillness to silence and silence to awakening. So, let all plans, worries, and all self-analysis, be still as you attend wholly to the saying of the word.

All thought tends to be connected with egoism and to activate self-consciousness, and that is why we let go of thoughts. We need to remind ourselves of this from time to time as we can slip into a lazy mode of meditation. In that mode we reduce the pure commitment to unselfconsciousness, and either watch the mind's meanderings or glean insights. In either case our fidelity to the mantra will be weakening. This will often be marked by the feeling that we have got everything we are going to get out of meditation. It is by no means a characteristic only of beginners.

As you sit there for these two half-hours of stillness each day – saying the mantra calmly, regularly, continuously – what happens? Thoughts will rush around you, racing each other, competing with each other to get your attention and trying to force you back into the race. Frequently they succeed, but briefly. So you continue quietly, despite all the thoughts, to return to the mantra. Somewhere, many times probably along this journey, you will have a sense of uneasiness, of missing something, of restlessness, a sense that you should be out there doing something, that you are wasting time, that you are losing your chances or position in the race. Life seems to be beating you. This feeling, however strong its anxiety level, has simply to be ignored.

It may be difficult to express or to understand at times why you are persevering, and even more difficult to make others understand why you are doing it. But as you persevere you come to realise that if there is no competition, there is no winning or losing. So what is there, we ask. Surely you have either got to win or lose. There is nothing else. But there *is* something else. When we see what that something else is, we have awakened.

The something else is a coming home, a being known. It is discovering love in the finding of your self. It is realising who you are, and what great gifts have been given to us all. What we are competing for has already been given us, freely as a gift. *Everything* is not something we have to compete for, but something we have to accept. That is the meaning of the Kingdom. When we enter the Kingdom within us we experience 'gift'. Competitiveness and ambition are linked to deep-rooted insecurities in the human psyche. As we meditate daily, with discipline leading us to freedom, we face these insecurities. We no longer evade them. Each of these insecurities we confront with the strength of unconditional and infinitely giving, love. The ego makes us seek to find and possess this love outside of ourselves. But meditation teaches us to find it at the centre of our selves. The fruit of interiority can never be possessed. And when the ego confronts unconditional giving it dissolves, ready to give itself up to the next stage of growth. Ultimately, it is the abundance of God's love, not his fullness but his overflowing, that inspires us to choose life, to choose growth.

Now that we have been justified through faith, let us continue at peace with God through Our Lord Jesus Christ, through whom we have been allowed to enter the sphere of God's grace, where we now stand. Let us exult in the hope of a divine splendour that is to be ours . . . because God's love has flooded our inmost heart through the Holy Spirit he has given us. (Rom. 5:1-2, 5)

Patterns and Identities

Somebody recently drew my attention to this sentence in John Main's book *The Present Christ*.

> If we live merely within the perspective of a fixed pattern from day to day, we are wasting our deepest response to life on what is passing away. We have not engaged with life on the level at which things endure.

She asked me wasn't meditation itself a 'fixed pattern'. Isn't daily meditation, the regular commitment we make to it, and the importance that we attach to doing it each morning and each evening, open to becoming just what it aims to liberate us from? Can't we see a subtle danger of entering into the 'perspective of a fixed pattern' which we are warned against? I began to reflect on that point and the light that it can shed on what it actually is we are doing when we meditate. It is not a new idea, of course. The desert Fathers were perhaps the first to warn against the danger of spiritual fanaticism and to propose, from the Christian viewpoint, the wisdom of moderation. Evagrius warned that the weapon against passion must not itself become a passion.

Meditation is very like entering a cave. If you ever spent any summer holidays by the sea as a child you probably went in search of caves along the coast. One day perhaps you found a cave and were thrilled by the adventure of finding it and the prospect of discovering pirate treasure inside. You are standing outside in the bright sunlight and suddenly the cave looks terribly, fearfully dark. But the darker it becomes, the brighter in your imagination becomes the treasure inside. You begin to enter the cave and a terrible fear wells up within you, as you project into its dark unknown all the unconscious fears in your own psyche. If you are very imaginative you see the monsters coming towards you from the dark. Yet you are irresistibly drawn onwards.

Meditation is very like that, a simultaneously irresistible and free entry into the unknown. We go a step further into the cave every time we meditate, not always with such dramatic fear, but always with an awareness that we are entering the unknown. We enter cave after cave, chamber after chamber, levels of reality, deeper and deeper, into the heart of reality where the treasure shines. It is always a going into the dark but 'the word of the Lord is a lamp for our steps'. The mantra is the light that we hold as we walk, and it dispels the darkness that evokes all fear.

The wonderful thing about meditation, the spiritual journey into the cave of the heart, is that once we have taken each successive step of faith and the light has shone in that dark place, then that place is enlightened. Fear, and the primal fear of death, is transcended. We are enlightened up to the point that we have reached on the journey. 'Everything', St Paul says, 'when once the light has shown it up is illumined and everything thus illumined is all light.' The inner chamber thus becomes increasingly filled with light as we take those repeated steps of faith, as we repeat the mantra, as we pursue the daily pilgrimage.

Meditation highlights in this way the relationship between what is passing away and what endures. What is passing away is the darkness and all the phantoms of the dark. What is enduring is the light that begins to shine. It is important to know how to relate both these levels of experience, the dark and the light, the enduring and the ephemeral because they are both to be lived with along the way. We need to be able to live our daily life rooted, as John Main said, on 'the level at which things endure . . . Each time we return to the changing pattern of our life we do so more firmly rooted in our being and so more able to perceive life as a mystery'.

Is that repetitive journey, that pattern of daily meditation, a 'fixed pattern'? Is it an inflexibility? Is it a narrowness? Not if we see it as the repetition of a step forward. Not if we understand the mystery of life as a cycle that repeats and yet advances, through repetition, to a new creation, to open new levels and explore new depths of life. Not if we can see that every time we move from what is eternal to what is passing away; and then as we return to the changing patterns of life, we do so more rooted in being. So I do not think our meditation is a 'fixed pattern'. It *is* a pattern. That is, it has a recognisable and constant identity. We do the same thing each day. But it is a moving pattern, and so we never really do the same thing each day. If you are building a house, each day you add a new brick. Meditation is not a fixed pattern in the way that we are often held by fixed patterns of fear, anger or compulsion. It is fixed only in the sense that it is something we persevere in. Or, in other words, it is faith. Faith is not fixity. It is not static. Faith is rooted in the eternal; but it is always changing the pattern within which it moves along.

What we can experience as an inflexibly fixed pattern is the state of egotism. Here is the fixed pattern it is vital we smash. It is crucial to life that we do not rationalise away, and do not evade this human work. We break the fixed grid of egoism by the energy of faith. Faith does not make sense, it does not make reality, unless it is repeated, unless it perseveres. What do we persevere in? And how is it that simple perseverance brings about an expansion in depth of life, consciousness and being? Faith is perseverance in the real identity that is ours, in the enduring identity that only commitment can reveal. Unless we are committed we have no constant identity. The ego is the self before it has found commitment in something beyond itself. Hegel said that we come to identify by immersing ourself in the other. Until we are fully immersed, then, fully committed, we will always be anxiously seeking ourselves. We seek those parts of our selves that remain islands of non-commitment, unsubmerged in the other.

The level at which we commit ourselves is the degree to which our identity is realised. If we are committed only to things at the level of egoism, our identity will not be realised beyond the level of the ego's shifting moods and masks. If we are committed to the values, and so to the challenges, of what is deeper than the ego, then an identity begins to emerge at the level of the true self. The form of our identity changes the more deeply we are committed, the more faithful we are. Even our nature changes as we meditate, daily, over the years. We become increasingly less self-conscious about the change that occurs within us because our very self-consciousness is disappearing. We know that we are changing, and we know it through the other, because we find ourselves more in love. We find ourselves acting less out of the fixed patterns of the ego and more out of the ever-expanding, and therefore indefinable, form of the true self. As we develop the unique and infinitely lovable identity that we have been given to find and realise, we discover ourselves becoming the person God chose before the world began.

It is like a waterfall. Somebody says to you, 'Come and see this beautiful waterfall.' You go and see it and you see incredible power, an immeasurable quantity of water, cascading down the mountainside. It is the waterfall they wanted you to see but it can never be the same waterfall. From moment to moment it changes. It is always changing, always new, always falling away from itself and yet rooted in its own identity. In that constant change there is a still certainty of identity. In faith, human consciousness is aware of this because faith brings us to the vision of what we truly are even as we become it. Without faith, we see only fixed patterns that are, in fact, decaying. By faith, we see expanding patterns that are evolving. We see the soul and we see that each person is a flowing stream of light. The identity of each infinitely lovable person is energy in a constant state of transformation. What we are being changed into now is what we will be for eternity, in the divine persons. We come to see by faith that each of us is a divine child of light.

In meditation we find the power that brings the constant change and daily transformation of human life to its highest development, because it roots it in a faith that opens up into consciousness. In meditation we find this power at our own source. We drink from our own wells. But we drink directly from the spring that feeds the well. We drink in the light of being from the Source from which light flows, the divine Spirit, the eternal spring of living water. The more deeply we drink, the more faithful we are, the more we become light. It is the earliest Christian discovery:

Here is the message that we heard from him and pass on to you: that God is light, and in him there is no darkness at all . . . If we walk in the light as he himself is in the light, then we share together a common life . . . The darkness is passing and the real light already shines. Christ has made this true and it is true in your own experience.   (1 John 1:5; 2:7, 8)

The Music of Being

At the beginning of the pilgrimage of meditation we are most concerned with coming to self-knowledge. This phase will see much psychological growth and the integration of much unresolved or evaded experience. But beyond a certain point, as there is less catching up with ourselves to accomplish, our concern shifts from self-knowledge to the knowledge of God. This is when the pilgrimage is really beginning and we realise that it is indeed a pilgrimage, not a race. A way of seeing the difference is to think of the beginning of a race with the runners all primed, their foot on the starting block. Racers run forward when the pistol cracks. Pilgrims run backwards using as much energy and skill as the racers, but making an absurd and scandalous counter-sign, a confusing clarification of the reason for running at all. At first we all run forward, seeking self-knowledge. Later we change direction, seeking God, leaving self behind.

The two forms of knowledge go together, of course. Christian tradition has always emphasised that if you want to know God you have to know yourself. You have to pass *through* self-knowledge to know God. These are not in fact two different goals or even two stages. They go together hand in hand. But it is important to understand, especially when you are beginning to meditate, that we are coming to a kind and a depth of self-knowledge that is unfamiliar to us. That is why the experience of meditation as a daily discipline is important, because it allows self-knowledge to become familiar and the new quality of it to become integrated with the ordinary. Meditation does not lead us only to self-knowledge but also to understand *how* we know ourselves. As we grow we become more critical of the models we employ to express the way that our being is interwoven of self-knowledge and the knowledge of God.

One of the models by which we are conditioned to understand ourselves is also one of the ways in which we are encouraged to develop ourselves: the mechanical model. We think of ourselves as some kind of machine, a super-computer, efficient, productive but, like all machines, disposable. The mechanical model is not very satisfactory. It leads to self-contempt and to the exploitation of others. It cannot account for the depths of human nature or the more wonderful qualities of our experience. Better than thinking of the human person as a machine we could think of ourselves as a piece of music, each person a whole piece of music and each piece a part of a greater symphonic whole.

Each of us is unimaginably complex. There are so many different functions going on at the same time, so many different dimensions within us, so many different levels of our being – neurological, physical, psychological, spiritual. This intricate, monumental complexity is hidden when we work in harmony. When all these different parts work together as they should, the harmony seems easy and effortless, like the performance of a great orchestra. It is rare that we are in a state of such complete harmony. Whenever this co-operation of all the parts is disrupted by psychological or by physical distress, then we see the different dimensions of ourselves suddenly fall apart and crash discordantly out of harmony. They lose their synchrony, the way they fit and work together. Each human being works as a whole, and to the degree that we do not work as a whole we do not work. We are like a piece of music played on many different instruments. Every instrument, however humble or small, has to play its significant part. If, as happens to all of us, we feel less than whole, if we feel a disharmony somewhere, a distress, a discontent, a depression or anxiety, then we need as the major priority of the moment to restore true musicality to our being.

If our inner music has been thrown into disharmony we need to restore it. We cannot run away from it without making it worse. If a part of the orchestra has never learned to play its instrument then it must learn. If a part of us has been overlooked or has never developed, it must be recognised and educated. How do we do that? How do we restore or introduce harmony into what has slipped out of truth? How do we discover what we really sound like? How do we find our true self?

And how do we understand to what, or to whom, our self is true?

Every spiritual tradition teaches meditation as the way. The rightness, the accurate tuning, the fullness, the music of being is restored by our coming into contact with a music beyond ourselves. We come into resonance with a harmony that is greater than our own interrupted harmony. We are drawn into completeness of harmony by *listening* to a deeper harmony. This listening is the meeting with the Holy Spirit, the Spirit of God that dwells within us and that, as St Paul says, 'comes to the aid of our weakness'. When we meditate we restore the lost, and repair the disrupted harmony of our being. We do that in the simplest and most powerful way. We do it, not by tinkering with our own instruments, not by self-analysis, but by listening to the deeper harmony of Christ – 'music heard so deeply that it is not heard at all.' T. S. Eliot's description captures the sense of loss and discovery in our relationship with Christ. Meditation is essentially about this listening. It is much more profound than listening with our ears, or concentrating with our minds. It is an obedient listening of the whole person. Indeed we come to wholeness by listening, fully and undistractedly.

Meditation is not a way of thought or analysis. Meditation is a way of attention, of pure, simple and total attention. Its discipline is to learn to listen wholeheartedly. Do not think that it is listening for a message. There is no message waiting to be beamed to us, telling us what lottery number to choose or whether to buy or sell. It is not for any kind of message like that, depriving us of freedom, that we are listening. Any words, images, or thoughts that come during the time of meditation we can safely regard as reflections from our own screen of consciousness. In prayer we go deeper than thoughts and deeper than all the mind's operations. We go, in all simplicity, in all gentleness because in all love, to the Spirit. The way we come to that attentiveness is by saying the mantra. The longer you say it, as the weeks, months and years go by, you will find that you are listening to it with more and more of your being.

The mantra is like a harmonic sounded deep within yourself that leads through all the disharmony, noise and distractions. Do not expect it to work immediately or miraculously. It is a work, a spiritual work, indeed, a discipline. But it is a sure, tested and a direct way. Saying the mantra clearly, articulating the word clearly in the centre of your being will teach you, among other things, what faith is. Say it clearly, gently, rhythmically, with both your mind and heart. Say it faithfully, however strong the distractions or disharmonies may be. Sometimes the distractions will be mental, at other times emotional. You will come to meditation each morning and evening with mental and emotional discordances, many arising from the disharmony of the worries of past, present or future. Say your mantra through it. Bring it to harmony.

There is nothing worse than feeling that we are 'bad music'. But often we can feel that we are ruled by something disharmonious, by the worst in ourselves; and often it is because we have tuned ourselves on something mediocre. There is nothing worse than feeling ruled by a tyranny of mediocrity. Musicians are always striving towards greater excellence in their playing. That is what we, as spiritual musicians, do when we meditate, and why we meditate every day regardless of whether we feel good or bad. By such discipline we avoid mediocrity. None of us wants to be essentially mediocre because none of us is mediocre.

Mediocrity refuses to allow a deeper harmony within us to expand beyond our disharmony. We remain mediocre by staying fixed on what is out of harmony, by concentrating on faults, failings or limitations. There is no reason for us to be fixed upon them, not when that deeper harmony of Christ exists within us. Growth happens whenever we listen to that deeper harmony. When, through meditation, we release it within ourselves we overflow with the music God plays in Christ. The mantra gently but surely transfers our attention from our disharmony to that deeper harmony and, in so doing, it brings us into harmony with itself and its source. As St Paul and the early Christians knew – and we have largely forgotten through mediocrity – this is the power that has changed the human condition:

> We ask God that you may receive from him all wisdom and spiritual understanding for full insight into his will, so that your manner of life may be worthy of the Lord and entirely

pleasing to him. We pray that you may bear fruit in active goodness of every kind, and grow in the knowledge of God. (Col. 1:9–10)

A Way of Life

The community of meditation groups around the world share a very central conviction. It is very simply the conviction that God is to be found at the centre of our personal being because the Spirit of Christ dwells within our hearts. The Christian has this 'mysterious' secret, to share with other Christians and with the whole world. The secret is Christ in us. Although it is a simple and not very intellectual conviction, it is one that gives an extraordinary depth and wonder to life. As a belief it goes right to the core of our being, literally. We can think about that conviction and we can discuss it, but only the experience of it ultimately means or verifies anything. By its nature, it is a simple belief and the experiential proof of it takes us through a process of simplification and on to ultimate unity. These small meditation groups are centres of this living faith and they are therefore able to share with all kinds of seekers the conviction that meditation is the way to the centre of our being. And, as such, it is the path to find Christ in us. His grace, his peace, his love, are part of that encounter. In the end it is a meeting, not a hearing, that persuades us.

It takes a certain time and there is a certain process involved in making this central conviction more than just one more interesting idea. It might be a very consoling idea. It might for some be a very intellectually stimulating idea. But it has to become more than an idea. It has to become a felt certainty. And in the teaching of John Main that convokes and inspires these groups you find a great emphasis on meditation as a process of conversion which is more than merely moral conversion. Indeed, moral conversion really happens 'after' this other conversion has begun, because this *basic* conversion is from theory to experience. Meditation is about that radical Christian conversion, a change from being people of theory, tasters of ideas, to people of experience, prophets of certainty.

This no doubt sounds rather arrogant. But in the course of that process, which does not happen overnight and yet which we can begin whenever we wish, all arrogance is burned away and we are compelled to become extraordinarily humble. But in process of becoming humble enough to accept the grace of Christ, we discover the childlike wonder and the innocent joy of being disciples. It is no small gift just to believe that we all are temples of the divine spirit. It is an even rarer gift to be able to believe it today, because it is not something that one is encouraged either to believe or confidently to proclaim in ordinary life. But it is the rarest – though not the most inaccessible – gift, to be able to *experience* ourselves and to see others as this temple. To believe and experience it reveals a mysterious certainty. It reveals the light in which we see light. It reveals faith.

The first thing the groups try to emphasise is that meditation is a way of experience not of thought. We have gradually to learn how to follow this way of non-thought, because we have been so conditioned to think and to think about thinking. It is as if the needle of consciousness got stuck in the groove of thought so that all our thoughts go round and round in circles. It is ultimately only experience that gently nudges the needle forward. We have to learn, perhaps to re-learn, the secret of non-thinking, of knowing reality directly and of experiencing the fullness of reality that is in the present moment. So much of our time is spent thinking about the past or dreaming about the future. If we are fully in the present moment, we are not dreaming or thinking, we are living. We do not have to try not to think. We only have to learn how to become present, how to be, now.

Thought is a rich and continual flow of consciousness in us. The present moment we are in is forever being remembered or anticipated. Often when we think we are in the present moment we are merely looking over the most recent pictures we have just had developed. There is an endless flow of ideas, clusters of ideas we call concepts, and of images. It all makes for a torrent of rational and imaginative consciousness. But there is a deeper level to this stream. It is a clearer, purer level where there are no thoughts or images and where we are already in a continual state of prayer. Here we are fully present, fully awake in the perpetual now. Meditation is about uncovering this level or depth of consciousness. The best way to answer the question 'What does meditation do?' is simply to say that it deepens us.

As soon as we begin to meditate we begin to discover this depth and slowly we learn to dwell there. At first, we discover it only briefly. Brief contact is made before you bounce back to the more agitated surface levels of the thoughts and images. Prayer is not about beachcombing the different levels of consciousness. It is not picking out shiny ideas or glittering experiences from the flotsom and jetsam carried along on the surface of the mind. When you are doing the *work* of meditation, see it always as a spiritual work of renouncing everything that is non-essential. During the actual times of meditation, all thoughts and all images, whatever their value, are non-essential distractions. With practice, and in time, we become more free through renunciation, and so more rooted in this deeper level. Meditation is not a fast technique of touching this depth and getting away with a quick experience. Meditation is a way of life that roots us in this depth-centre continuously. The only purpose of prayer is to lead us into the state of continual prayer.

I said it is a way of life. This is because it applies faith and values that we would die for and therefore that make life worth living for. Meditation applies these felt certainties at the level of pure being, so that they can become life-enhancing, redemptive realities in action as well. Any such way of life is a discipline that requires perseverance. Meditation is a special kind of way and so asks a special kind of discipline. Meditation is the discipline that teaches us discipline and it requires a fidelity that teaches us how to be faithful. It is so, because it is pure experience. That is why the moral conversion of all aspects of life happens as a result of this pure experience.

How do we enter this pure experience at depth and with clarity? We enter it through the discipline of the mantra. The mantra is a simple and traditional way which leads us beyond thoughts and images. It is as simple as you find it to be when you do it for the first time. It is very difficult, though, to believe that its most persuasive characteristic will always be just this difficult simplicity. You need to keep returning to the mantra continually during the meditation as soon as you are aware that you have stopped saying it. But you will find that your awareness will bob back to the surface of your thoughts and images even when you have decided to be faithful to the mantra. Keep saying the mantra. It does not matter what thought comes into your mind, whether it is interesting, good or bad, or what picture and images pass across the screen of consciousness. Nor does it matter how many times you unconsciously forget this and get waylaid by the fascinating treasure-house of sublimities and trivia that mental consciousness contains. It does not even matter if you get discouraged and feel the whole attempt is futile. It is like walking. If you want to arrive, do not stop. Keep putting one foot in front of the other. Or like swimming, keep doing one stroke after the other.

The other face of the discipline is to meditate every day. That is above all what makes it a way of life rather than just a technique to quick experience. To meditate twice a day is a challenge and a major new life-discipline. But there is hardly any point in trying to do a little bit of meditation. It requires regularity and steadiness. It may take time to build this discipline into your life, so give yourself plenty of time. Be patient with your impatience. But remember also there is no point in wasting time once you have decided to begin. Set aside the half an hour each morning and evening as if it were a gift of time you were giving to someone else, not as something for your own enjoyment or benefit. See it as a kind of tithing of your time.

What makes meditation a pure experience is that there is nothing secondhand in it. It is not anyone else's experience. You are not competing with anyone else. You are not competing with St John of the Cross, Suzuki, Merton or Main, or with anyone who has ever gone before. Nor are you comparing yourself with anyone else. That is why it is neither comparable nor measurable. That is why it is about finding your own self. The only measure is the simpler, greater depth and intensity of the life we find ourselves living. The early monks described the mantra as leading to 'purity of heart' by way of poverty of spirit. The pure of heart see God, and this is the meaning of happiness and blessedness. Meditation is a way of joy. The fullness and expansiveness of being, that accompany joy, are infinitely greater than whatever we usually think of as happiness. To live fully we have to learn what life is about. We have to discover what fullness of life really is. Meditation will teach us.

It teaches us through a subtle but comprehensive change in the way we respond to life. This is the real conversion. We then learn to see that happiness is not so much doing what we like as liking what we do. It teaches us that the measure of happiness is not wanting what we see, but seeing what we want. The pure experience in meditation teaches us that it is not in seeing any *thing* that we see God, but simply in the seeing. Joy is pure clear perception of what is, undistorted by egoism and undistracted by selfconsciousness. It is a great claim to make for meditation, for the mantra, but it is one that experience will verify personally, for anyone who will trust themselves to this way.

In the words of Scripture, 'Things beyond our seeing, things beyond our hearing, things beyond our imagining, all prepared by God for those who love him', these it is that God has revealed to us through the Spirit.   (1 Cor. 2:9–10)

The Union of Opposites

Life can offer many types of feelings in a very short period of time. Naturally, we fear the fading of the pleasant ones and the onset of the unpleasant. All we can be sure of, though, is that they are cyclical. The cycle of our emotions is driven by the wheel of multiplicity, of change and of fortune. A certain detachment, which does not have to be cold insensitivity or chilly stoicism, is an almost inevitable accompaniment to the maturing process of the first (seventy-five or so?) years of life. We need not look too much to our emotions alone to yield the secret of life's meaning. Perhaps the only feeling we should be very seriously concerned about is the feeling of boredom. If we feel bored there is something radically wrong with life. We have blocked the flow from one pole of experience to the other. Experience is full of opposites. And the fundamental interest of life, indeed the vitality of life, is the shift from seeing opposites as contradictions to seeing them as paradoxes.

While they are merely contradictions we know disharmony and anxiety, and we have to cope with life as a series of problems. We even encounter our self as a problem to be solved. As the changing life-process teaches us how to see – and so how to live – we begin to turn contradictions into paradoxes. These are opposites that complement each other, that balance us and achieve credible wholeness, not unconvincing answers. We begin to see life and ourselves, not as a complex problem to be solved, but as a mystery to be entered into.

One of the great paradoxes of growth, which explores what life is about, is that growth occurs when there is a combination of opposites, for example, rootedness and expansion, stillness and movement. While we view them only as contradictions it seems we have to decide between them. We feel like Solomons in judgement over our solitary lives. One of the essential ways that we grow, and one of the things that we should not avoid or delay, is through decision. Every day presents us with a vast number of decisions, some of which we take automatically, others which we agonise over. Even if we avoid those decisions, we have taken a decision, a decision not to decide, to avoid them. Nevertheless, however important it is to learn to decide, it is also important to let be, to allow contradictions to evolve into life-giving paradoxes.

Decisions are always important in shaping life and in revealing its meaning, depth and quality. It is like the decision we have made to meditate. The modern problem is that there are so many decisions to be made. So many possible options are open to us and we want to make the one, right and only decision, in order to be true to ourselves. Yet faced with such an overwhelming number of possibilities to choose between, truth can easily become trivialised. Truth, which is both right and appropriate, can become reduced to one answer in a kind of multiple-choice exam. The modern problem in deciding to meditate or in taking any other serious decision is that we fear losing our other options. How do we know that multiple-choice 'B' might not be just as good as multiple-choice 'Z'. Also, we fear intensely, as modern people, that if we become fully committed to one particular, we lose the absolute and universal that we seek and thirst for. We have lost the wisdom of simpler societies and peoples who know that the universal is only found in and through the particular. In our materialism, and in our decadence, we have become so much more abstract. But the decision to meditate is redemptive because it teaches this simple wisdom in a way we find credible, that is a practical and experiential way.

The decision to meditate teaches that our immediate concern should not be with the results of our decision. 'What is going to happen as a result of my choosing this particular, rather than that?' Such a question reveals a highly abstract concern. We should be less concerned with what is going to happen than with the whole-heartedness with which we make and pursue the decision. We should be concerned about the quality, the depth, of faith. Every decision is an act of faith.

We should also be concerned about the most important consequence arising from any act of faith, which is our perseverance in that decision. To persevere in a decision is as important as taking it. Faith is meaningless without perseverance. Faith without fidelity is mere experimentation. The mantra teaches us in the simplest of all ways, and through the simplest of all experiences, how to make a decision rightly. It teaches us to be people of faith. Perhaps more than anything else this is why it has such a profound effect on our lives as a whole.

Meditation soon teaches us that perseverance is not the same as obstinacy. it is not about rigidity. Faith is always flexible, because it seeks always to be true to the same decision in different circumstances. Where does *rightness* enter? If we are making the decision in the right way then it will be the right decision. If we are making it faithfully, and that means persevering in it, then we can be sure of one thing, with the certainty of faith, that rootedness in that act of faith will lead to growth. We need not try to predict what is going to happen as a result of a decision because the circumstances of life are themselves changed once we have made it. The most significant and creative thing we can do in life is to make decisions of faith. Circumstances will change as the carpet of reality continues to unroll. Reality always surprises us, but always with what we come to see as recognisable events or qualities. Enlightenment is a homecoming. Reality is unconventional but it establishes true order. The decision of faith changes the circumstances of life just as self-knowledge changes the person we are. When we know ourselves, then we are no longer the person we were. When we are living in reality, no longer in fear, desire or fantasy, we are in a new creation.

It is always the same faith that we are exercising, the same innate personal quality of humanness. There are different forms and expressions of it, but always the same faith proceeding from the deepest centre of personal identity and making us more and more the person we are. Commitment to the consequences of a decision and persevering in the primary act of faith leads us to progressive transformation. The great transformation is the transforming of our selves into higher levels of being. We are always wanting to change externals but the important thing to change is ourselves.

The growth that results from these acts of faith, these multiple expressions of a single act of faith in life, are not only concerned with the environment in which our identity develops. They are concerned with the essence of who we are. Everywhere in the Gospel the message rings out clearly. 'It is by faith that you are saved. It is faith that makes you whole . . . Your faith has healed you. Faith moves mountains.' An essentially Christian way to understand the mantra is as a pure and simple act of faith. It is like an anchor that keeps us rooted through the storms of growth. It is like a polestar, the fixed point that allows us to steer a true course. It is also like the oars of the boat propelling us forward with the current, with the tide, our spirit finding and co-operating with the Spirit of God.

We may ask what we are growing into. What is this 'conversion' process leading to? What is this transformation for? The Gospel tells us that it is into Christ that we are growing and changing and being transformed. 'The life I live is no longer my own life, but the life that Christ lives in me.' This is life we live, by faith, *in Christ*. The transformation of identity occurs through the loss of the ego, of our clinging to separateness and our refusal of personhood. Our awakening is to the non-duality of our relationship with Christ.

Modern psychiatry understands wholeness as the union of opposites. It allows us to understand, in a way that as modern people we can find credible, what holiness is and to see holiness as the awakening of that personal centre where we are fully present in our own centre of gravity. To be whole is to be conscious at that centre of the self where all the extremes of personality are balanced. From whatever end of the spectrum we may start the journey of meditation, we are always moving towards the centre. This common direction and goal explains the universal community of the spirit, and why so many different types can meet while travelling to that same centre from such different starting points. The pilgrimage explains love as the way in which the distance between the starting points is transcended in a unity of purpose, which is to be at one with the centre of the deepest of centres, with Christ. Meditation reveals what life is like 'in Christ', as a life of other-centredness, open to the other and, so, to the essential paradox that it is only by being rooted in the other that we can be fully alive.

The mystery of Christ living in us is that it empowers us to experience God in others. It opens us to perhaps the most surprising aspect of reality, and also one of the most joyfully recognisable, that we find the deepest joy, not in an egotistical search for God, but by seeing others find God. We will be most free and most full when we delight in the growth and wholeness of others. The contemplative experience is thus the maker of the church-experience as described by its early witnesses:

Your life in Christ makes you strong, and his love comforts you. You have fellowship with the Spirit, and you have kindness and compassion for one another. I urge you, then, to make me completely happy by having the same thoughts, sharing the same love, and being one in soul and mind. Don't do anything from selfish ambition or from a cheap desire to boast, but be humble towards one another, always considering others better than yourself. And look out for one another's interests, not just for your own. The attitude you should have is the one that Christ Jesus had. (Phil. 2:1–5, TEV)

Gift

Whoever wants their life to be fully alive, fully human, needs to have a spiritual path. We need a spiritual discipline which we can integrate into daily life as a central priority. A characteristic of any discipline is that you are regular in your practice of it. Yet we live a life full of irregularities, full of unpredictable events and changes of mood. One day you feel very spiritual and meditating is the easiest thing in the world; the next day you feel very fleshly and you do not want to meditate, you just want to watch TV or go shopping. Then there are the unpredictable things that happen, not only your moods, but changes of plans, crises, or somebody coming to see you at the wrong time. Then it seems very difficult to live an ordinary life and to keep a regular spiritual discipline. Monasteries only exist because the irregularity of life makes spiritual discipline so difficult. When they are feeling humble, monks will recognise themselves, at least in part, as people who could live a spiritual life in no other way. But their weakness makes them a strong witness to what everyone is meant to do: to live with God as the centre of your life as well as of your ideology.

There are certain times of the year when irregularity increases and everything gets even more hectic than usual. The pressures upon you become greater and probably, although not necessarily, the first thing to go is your spiritual discipline. These are useful occasions to test the seriousness of the spiritual commitment in your life. Christmas, for example, is a time of the year when, above all, we should be aware of the presence of the Spirit. The whole meaning of Christmas, of the human coming of God in Jesus, is that we should be more mindful of the Presence amid the ordinary routines and concerns. It is a time of the year, therefore, when the challenge to the discipline of daily meditation can reveal a great deal about how firmly we are on our pilgrimage.

Christmas is a time of the year, too, when we should become deeply aware of the gift of meditation. We may know that there is a spiritual path to follow, we may deeply and seriously want to follow it; but it is a great gift to be given the way to follow it. To understand meditation as a gift is perhaps the best of all ways to be faithful to the discipline that it asks of us. The discipline is of meditating every day, even on Christmas Day, even on Christmas Eve.

It is a time of the year when we are encouraged to give. Or rather, it is a time of the year when we are encouraged to buy so that we can give. It is not only in giving, however, that we are generous. If we are committed to the spiritual discipline we have a very valuable gift to *receive*, to receive more and more generously. We are generous in the way we receive as well as the way we give. With the gift of meditation we have a great means to help us avoid becoming absorbed in the commercialism of a consumer-culture that reaches such a peak at this once religious time of the year. We are given the opportunity, in receiving this spiritual gift, to reflect on the nature of existence, as a whole, as pure gift.

To see life as a spiritual reality requires more than reflection and thought. It requires a certain depth of experience. Only experience ultimately persuades. To become rooted in the experience of gift is a prerequisite for any spiritual awareness. And to be rooted in it, we need to see or experience it more than once. We need to return to it regularly and faithfully. Repetition, and the impossibility of repeating anything exactly, lies at the heart of the truth of religion. This is why religion is closer to the deeper truths of the cycle of people's lives than politics, philosophy or economics. Religious repetition is the meaning of the regularity of meditation. Each time we return to it, whatever our mood, whatever our agenda, we are rooting ourselves more deeply in the reality of the Spirit.

When we think about the gifts we have received, the mind usually turns to the things that 'make me happy' now, the things that I wanted and by skill or fortune managed to acquire. But this is fairly superficial. It is not just what we are given or win, or the lucky things that happen that is gift, but it is who we *are*, the very fact that we are at all. This is essentially the nature of gift: existence itself. That is the gift that really needs to be experienced, the givenness, the grace, the gift of personal being.

Whenever we receive a gift, or sense that we are recipients of something unearned, the natural response, if we are open to it, is to thank the giver. But how do you thank the one who gives you the very capacity to be grateful? The greater the gift, the more speechless our gratitude. We thank the giver of the gift of being, by being. By being who we are, we allow ourselves to become the person we are called to be. The regular practice of meditation opens the centre of personal being to a spirit of thanksgiving, to a joy. We are perhaps most unselfconsciously joyful when we are sincerely giving thanks. Joyfulness of being is the fruit of rootedness in the experience of being as gift; and that root of unselfconscious gratitude goes to the very ground of our being.

We call it reverence, awe and wonder. The root of thanksgiving goes infinitely deeper than the unpredictable and irregular elements of life. It goes deeper than moods or events. It sinks consciousness into the sure ground on which life, with all its fluctuations, is built. Meditation releases a pent-up energy of joy, in what a Christian might call the ontological eucharist of prayer. Meditation will not wave a magic wand over the things in your life that you would rather get rid of. What it does, is to deepen the ground upon which you stand to live your life. To know ourselves as given to ourselves (and others) is the experience of prayer, and it is one that takes us beyond ourselves. It may sound rather self-centred to emphasise this knowledge of ourselves as being given to ourselves. But if we really enter into the experience, then we find that we are, already, going beyond ourselves. Before we know where we are, we are going beyond self-consciousness into the knowledge of the person who bestows the gift. Knowing ourselves as gift is the beginning of the experience of God.

When this experience has begun, it begins to rearrange our whole value system, because right at the centre of that system, which decides how we actually live, there is now the knowledge and experience of gift. We cannot be possessive about a gift. If we try to possess it, it ceases to be a gift and becomes a possession. If we accept a gift and hold it reverently as something unearned and wondrous, we become as free as the gift itself. Because the greatest quality of a gift is that it mediates its own freedom to us; when we learn how to receive, we become non-possessive in all ways and relationships. Here is one of the reasons that the most important and enduring fruit of meditation is not to be found in what happens during the times of meditation. The real fruit you will become aware of through relationships, and a new sense both of presence and of purpose. It will be from the people you are in relationship with that you will learn most clearly what is happening in yourself.

The greatest gift is that we are able to know ourselves as gift and therefore to know the Giver. Jesus calls that gift the experience of the Kingdom and he describes it as being like a treasure buried in a field, or a pearl of great price. Once we have glimpsed this treasure, this hidden gift, we are prepared to sell everything we possess in order to enjoy it fully. That is what we do when we meditate. We give up everything we *have*, to be everything we *are*. To say the mantra is precisely a letting go of everything that we have acquired in any way, and of everything that we still want to acquire that is present imaginatively in our desires. It is the letting go of possessions that enables us to receive and enjoy the gift. The mantra's work is the uncovering of the gift.

Work and faith are needed to unearth and disclose the buried treasure. It is important for us, if we are to approach meditation seriously, to understand prayer as work, as a real work of our spirit, in the Spirit. But it is a curious type of work because most work we are used to tires us whereas the work of the Spirit renews, energises and refreshes us. It does not mean that because it refreshes us, it is not work. It may be the hardest work when it refreshes us most. Saying the mantra is not easy – the letting go of thoughts, of desires, of all fantasies, problems and anxieties. It is a letting go of everything. That is not easy because, even if we do not cling to them, they often cling to us.

The mantra makes it possible to come to that total simplicity of being humble and grateful, in the reception of the supreme gift of life and consciousness. Sometimes we have to dig through a lot of rubble, down through the quarries of the past, through layers of repression and illusion, and through great quantities of distraction that are not only generated by ourselves, but also unconsciously absorbed from everything around us. But recovering the gift-experience, finding this treasure buried in our own inner field, is a healing work.

Gift

Through this work we re-enter a state of innocence. Innocence is beautifully symbolised by the giving and the receiving of a gift in a reciprocal directness of experience, where we are not concerned about analysing our feelings or what the other person is feeling. We are not complicating complexity more, but discovering that primary state of innocence in which we enter events, places and people directly and unselfconsciously. The way to come to that happy state is to say the mantra with real fidelity. The early monks said that if you knew that you were praying, then you were not really praying. What they meant by that is something very challenging to people of our culture who like to know all the time what they are doing and thinking, and who like to record the experience as it happens.

Unselfconsciousness is a very challenging idea but one that meditation authenticates. To be able to go beyond the limitations imposed upon us by self-awareness is like untying the rope that keeps us bound to a fixed stake. The mantra unpicks the knot with sharp and nimble precision, and loosens us into an, at first, dizzying universe of freedom. The gift of being is the reason for accepting the yoke of saying the mantra continually during the time of the meditation. There will always be a tendency to go back, to try to experience the experience or to possess the gift. But if we are saying and returning to the mantra continually, we transcend that tendency and enter the state of freedom.

Singlemindedness, as the way to expansiveness, is what Jesus called setting the mind upon the Kingdom before everything else, focusing the whole person in the centre of being. The mantra introduces us to the paradox of this. It is the paradox that finding is impossible without losing. You have to lose something in order to find. Accepting the gift is impossible without letting go. The mantra is what enables us to find and to accept. Another wonder of the great gift that Jesus has given us in himself is the gift of peace. It is one that bestows freedom from fear and, with freedom, we are able to see and know everything, even our selves and each other, as the gift of God.

Peace is my parting gift to you, my own peace, such as the world cannot give. Set your troubled hearts at rest, and banish your fears.   (John 14:27)

69

The Gift of Fullness

Even when someone has been meditating for only a short time, he or she soon discovers that meditation is simpler than it looks, but not as easy as it sounds. It sometimes strikes me that it might be better if meditation could be made more complex, because it would then be easier. Easier to begin and to persevere. But it really is the simplicity of meditation that is its great power. The power that faith releases is the power to simplify us and so bring us to that unity which we most long for. Unity gives us the primary and needed experience of being whole. I suppose all the experiences in our range of feeling or knowledge are characterised by impermanence, but one of the most fleeting of all is that of total completeness. It is very rarely and briefly that we know plenitude, fullness of being, an integrated sense of well-being, harmony and balance, where every need that we have is met and every desire that troubled us is forgotten. Of all moments, these are perhaps the most fleeting experiences of life. Usually they happen to us quite unexpectedly. They are unpredictable and usually have little to do directly with what we have just been desiring. In fact, the nature of the joy soon leads one to suspect that getting what is desired is not at all an experience of completeness. Mere satisfaction is not nearly as genuinely fulfilling as those unpredictable occurrences of pure gift.

When we do know this completeness, when by some incredible chance it all seems to come together (although chance never adequately explains it and there is always a sense of purpose and higher meaning within it), we rediscover a new innocence. A clarity and a simplicity of being, that makes all our former complexity seem absurdly irrelevant, suddenly reigns. All the anxious straining and effort to gain completeness are made redundant and irrelevant. What we regain, at a higher level of maturity, is the lost quality of a child. But these experiences of completeness are transient, and the more we try to hold on to them the quicker they fade. That is a truth you may have already discovered with regard to meditation in particular. Sometimes in the early stages of learning to meditate you can find yourself coming into a state of deep peace, a sense of fullness, calm, well-being and joy. Within a milli-second of noticing it and enjoying it, you begin to wonder how long it will last. And then it is gone. If you try to recall it by remembering it, that only pushes it further back. It is all a very valuable lesson of how every bestowal of completeness is pure grace, pure gift. We for our part must learn how to receive them graciously. The moment the ego tries to throw the net of ownership over them we find ourselves caught in that net and our freedom-loving Ariel has flown. The more we try to repeat these experiences the rarer they become.

Meditation here focuses on one of the most universal elements of human life, which is our more or less constant sense of incompleteness. It is often a vague sense of something lost or missing, or of something expected and waited for. It is better to leave it indeterminate than to project it on to particular fantasies of happiness. Yet often we try to escape its insistent presence by identifying it with some superficial desire or ambition. If we do happen to succeed in fulfilling that desire or achieving that ambition, we soon discover that it has not really assuaged the deeper ache. It has not addressed that strangely hopeful sense of incompleteness. Whenever we take the risk to be more conscious, or give the time for a need deeper than desire to emerge, we immediately step aside from the convergent forces of our particular lifestyle and culture, that are always threatening us with boredom, oblivion or burnout. If we ever are still enough to face ourselves at all, we must encounter this incompleteness.

One of the great problems of modern lifestyles is just how intense the pain of this perennial human sense of incompleteness can become. This is largely because it is the needing area of the self that is most callously manipulated and exploited by the consumer society which imprisons us all, rich and poor, to one degree or another. With a demonic impersonality it feeds on people's needs. Its economic greed wants and plots to keep us all in a permanent state of incompleteness and of whetted appetite. It is not insignificant that advertising, the smiling mask of this demon, so exploits the sexual imagination which contains the symbols of our most vulnerable longings for wholeness. The modern sense of incompleteness has been so intensified by such exploitation because our experiences of completeness have become so rare. We are now so unprepared for the exquisitely simple ways in which the gift of completeness arrives. We are so complex and self-conscious that we lack the spontaneity, the nimble childlikeness, to recognise or respond when the moment of grace comes. We are so sceptical that we rarely trust the gift or the process of simplification that leads to the gift. If for no other reason, this is why it is so vital for modern people to learn to meditate.

Meditation is the ancient and universal practical wisdom, the way to learn the most important human qualities, to be simple, free, trusting and faithful. Meditation works, firstly, by leading us to face ourselves as we are; and probably we are gravely deficient in all these qualities. Meditation calls us back from the fantasy, pessimism and distraction in which we so often lose and waste ourselves. We are called back to *be* ourselves. Here is the first and most simple thing that meditation does. Learning to know ourselves, not just to *think* about ourselves, because we think about ourselves and our needs quite enough. When it comes to the times of meditation we are not thinking about ourselves. We are *being* ourselves.

There is a story from the west of Ireland that captures the difficulties of self-knowledge. It is about a simple farmer living on a remote island who rowed into town one day. In a shop there he found a mirror which was something he had never seen before. He picked up the mirror, looked into it and saw his face. Not knowing what it was, he said, 'My God, it's a picture of my father!' So he bought the mirror and took it home with him. He did not want his wife to see it and kept it hidden. But occasionally she would see him looking secretly at this object. She was sure it was a picture of a rival for her affections, some other woman he had met in town. So one day when he was away she took out his box and found where he had hidden the mirror. She looked in it, saw herself and cried aloud with relief, 'Who's this ugly old hag? No competition there!' And she replaced the twice-misunderstood mirror of self-knowledge.

We rarely recognise ourselves when we see ourselves as we

really are. Coming to self-knowledge is more demanding, and requires more insight, than just looking at the surface and responding to an image of ourselves. It is essential for completeness that we do come to self-knowledge. The Christian tradition has always insisted that we must first know ourselves before we can come to know God. St Augustine prayed, 'May I know myself so that I may know You.' In coming to know ourselves we have simply to learn to *be* ourselves. That includes our incompleteness, our unflattering similarity to others and our unique blemishes. Accepting ourselves as we are makes us capable of the gift of wholeness. Above all, in meditation we are learning, not to judge ourselves as successes or failures by comparison with this person or that social image or that commercial idyll, but simply to be who we are.

How does meditation do this most simple but most important of all human works? It does it by positioning us firmly in the present moment. By teaching us to be *now* it teaches us to be only ourselves. It takes some time to learn to be now. But as we learn it in those two periods of meditation every day we carry that natural skill into the rest of life. A fruit of meditation is learning to be more and more present in every action and situation. In this subtle but integrative way meditation changes your life. The first thing it teaches is to stop thinking of the past or of the future, indeed to stop thinking at all. It does so by our learning to say the mantra with wholehearted attention at the centre of our being.

It is all-important to grasp the centrality of the mantra. There are no techniques of any real significance to learn in meditation. The only thing to learn is to say the mantra as faithfully, as continuously as you can, from the beginning to the end of each meditation. Meditation leads to wholeness by teaching us that we do not complete ourselves. No skill, no acquisition, no achievement, or possession can complete us. Meditation conveys the great and universal spiritual wisdom that we do not find this longed-for completeness by acquiring anything but by losing something. We lose it, we evolve beyond the ego with all its complexity and possessiveness, in the simple saying of the word. The mantra responds to the essential teaching of Jesus that whoever wishes to find his life, must lose it.

In the Christian vision, by letting go, we move into the completeness of Jesus. His risen life is wholly present in his

Spirit within us. The way of meditation is open to everyone because everyone is graced by this Spirit of wholeness. Every human being is equal on the path of meditation and every human being is called to completeness. This is the essential truth of the gospel:

> So shall we all at last attain to the unity inherent in our faith and our knowledge of the Son of God – to mature humanity, measured by nothing less than the full stature of Christ. (Eph. 4:13)

Traction and Distraction

At the beginning of anything new, like a new year, a new job or new way of life, we all need personal encouragement. Always a good way to encourage each other to be faithful to the ever-new path of meditation is to address the ways in which we get *dis*couraged.

One of the discouragements is to see ourselves as less generous, less loving, less selfless than we would like to be and than we know we should be. Another way in which we get discouraged is the persistence of distractions as we find ourselves, particularly at the time of meditation, still scattered and unfocused. St Paul knew that the great value of community lay in telling the truth to each other and encouraging each other on the way of growth. He has been talking about the ways that one should order one's life when he says this to the Corinthian church:

> In saying this I have no wish to keep you on a tight rein. I am thinking simply of your own good, of what is seemly, and of your freedom to wait upon the Lord without distraction. (1 Cor. 7:35)

The experience of distraction is not peculiar to ourselves as modern people. Everyone who has ever tried to follow the Way of Christ, like everyone who has ever tried to meditate, has discovered distraction. As we persevere on the way we can sometimes pass through what seem like depressingly endless stretches of consciousness where there seems to be nothing but distraction. We try to concentrate, we sit down with every intention to give full attention to the mantra. But despite the good intention, despite having tried to do it many hundreds of times before, we still drift off. It is like trying to hold on to something with a hand in which the muscles are too weak. The most important practical attitude that we have to learn in order to remain faithful to meditation is how to deal with the distractions. Because they are going to be fairly constant companions.

At first we can try to deal with them by suppressing them, as if using the mantra to hammer them down. We try to force the gates of the Kingdom. But as we go on, as the teaching with its simplicity and its wisdom of gentleness begins to sink into us, we learn that distractions are best dealt with by *not trying* to deal with them. This means allowing the mantra to deal with them, which it does by the gradual, accumulative effect of its influence of faith. We never pass beyond distraction by giving attention to the flow of distractions. There is the first of the most important lessons that we have to learn. We have to stop thinking about our distractions, to stop turning our attention to them, because that only increases them and exacerbates their influence. To go through them, to cross over the ground of consciousness that we must cover in order to reach our destination, we pay attention only to the mantra. With a steadily deepening faith. And the deepening of that faith is love.

This process of deepening leads to unexpected levels of self-knowledge. They are unimagined. They come upon us like unexpected messengers. We come to the self-knowledge of humility, not as a result of focusing the intellect or psychological introspection upon the contents of consciousness but by turning the attention of consciousness off ourselves. We learn most effectively when we learn indirectly. In this, as in the other ways by which we become humble, we discover natural laws that surprise us by being more efficient than the mental tools that we think of as the most effective. The mantra, even after many years, remains a very surprising discovery.

The first stages of self-knowledge are usually perceived as negative. We come to recognise our potential by experiencing our limitations. But this negative self-knowledge, knowing our faults, our failures, our limited capacities and talents, is only a stage. It may involve suffering. It may even take us to meet the great temptation of despair where we feel we cannot progress because we cannot be loving and we cannot be more attentive. But what seems negative gradually becomes a positive self-knowledge as the sense of limitation gently and surprisingly changes into the awareness of our potential in Christ. As ideas and images of Christ give way to his emergent self-revelation as someone to be known, loved and trusted, we sense that in which his personal reality actually exists. In him, human limitation has transcended itself without ceasing to be human. By knowing him we become humanly divine. In the state of isolation from which Christ has delivered us we look upon ourselves with the limited vision of the ego. We see only limitation. But when we can see ourselves in Christ, we see infinite possibility. This is the experience that lies behind Simone Weil's saying 'that the only way to overcome our limitations is to accept them'.

If we do indeed find God in a place beyond distraction it is the place which is nowhere and everywhere, because it is pure experience. It is the place which is the Kingdom within. As we learn to recognise the spiritual locus of this place we approach it with an ever greater spirit of attention, which combines wonder with freedom and humility. The effect of that on daily life is to set loose great forces of compassion and generosity. Freedom to wait upon the Lord without distraction is its great sign. Then even waiting becomes joyful. Hope becomes creative and meaningful.

As we draw closer to this place of union, it is the mantra which pulls us through the distractions that keep us separate. The sense of being 'pulled' through, of being led, of following and of making progress, is essential to the Christian understanding of the Way. The word *distraction* itself says something about the Way. It is the opposite of 'traction', which is the action of drawing or pulling. It conveys the sense of the process of advancing, of movement, through contact with another surface. Traction means the grip that a wheel must have on a surface in order to turn. If faith is the grip, Christ is the surface. Distraction is the loss of this grip. It is the loss of direction to consciousness. So it is the end of being drawn forward and the end of all real movement or growth. It is the beginning of aimless drifting.

We all begin distracted and this is the best way to understand original sin. But the traction of the mantra pulls the turning wheel out of its rut. It restores direction by focusing consciousness and giving it direction and purpose. This focusing is such a momentous reclarification that it is like a new awakening to the world. In place of the three-dimensional world of limited reality we perceive the infinitely-dimensional Kingdom through the enlightenment Christ sheds in our heart and mind.

As we follow this way of integration we may at times feel paradoxically that we are disintegrating. The traction of the mantra can even seem like distraction. People sometimes say they could concentrate on God more directly without the bother of the mantra. Is all this effort really worth it? Do I really have to give so much to the journey? Surely the Lord does not demand this much? Aren't I missing out on something? But at first we have got everything reversed and our responses are unreliable. While they are being straightened out we may sometimes become more confused. We forget which way round we should be, which way round we are. We have to get our bearings. The process of integration, of unification, of simplification, demands perseverance. Without it there is no journey. It is a perseverance composed of a living spirit of faith, an energy which is always a mystery to us because it is the energy of grace, a gift beyond our control or possession. This gift of faith is the gift to persevere in deepening love and in ever greater generosity.

It is specifically faith in the presence of Jesus. Certainly there is for many the *belief* that he is present within us. But there is also the *faith* that is gained by being, perhaps unawares, in his presence. The hidden but still objective influence of his presence in our deepest being leads to the real faith that Christ is found in the place of no distraction. There, in and with him, we find God. The place beyond distraction exists within us and the gate into it is open. This is the great news that we have to share with the world. It exists and is open within us because Jesus, the One without distraction, has his consciousness utterly attentive to God and to us simultaneously.

So St Paul can say earlier in the letter to the Corinthians that 'there is no place for human pride in the presence of God. You are in Christ Jesus by God's act, for God has made him our wisdom; he is our righteousness; in him we are consecrated and set free' (1 Cor. 1:29–30).

The Way and Its Ways

The most powerful time people can spend together is that spent in deep, confident silence. In preparation for that the meditator becomes increasingly familiar with the spiritual tradition which puts us on the way of silence and expands our understanding of its significance. In the extended spiritual *familia* of Christian meditation groups, the guiding tradition derives from within the Christian monastic, Benedictine lineage. But it is essentially a universal tradition. No order or school of spirituality can claim ownership of what the Spirit freely bestows through different gifts on all. In every major religious tradition there is what is known as a 'path' that teaches the way of silence. A path is a more or less systematised or coherent sense of the process and pattern of spiritual growth.

The path is a sense of the pattern we undergo and participate in as we come to full humanity and into being the person that we are meant to be. In China, this path is called the Tao, in Buddhism the Eightfold Path, in Judaism the Law. In Christianity this path was originally called, very simply, the Way. And the first Christian communities called themselves 'followers of the Way'. What is unique about the Christian path is that its Way is not a set of moral commands, philosophical or ethical truths or cultic observances. It is not a set of laws, but a *logos*. It is not a set of philosophical truths, but a *wisdom*. It is not even a set of religious beliefs, but *faith*. The more specifically religious characteristics of Christianity developed after the brief period of direct experience of the Resurrection. Today they are inherited and must be pierced through before we come to that direct experience.

Essentially, the Way for a Christian is a real person. The Truth of the Way is wholly *embodied* in the human person of Jesus. So, to be following the Way is something more than studying a religious system of beliefs. To be a disciple of the

79

Way is more than obeying certain moral or religious laws. It is a whole form of life which is not merely cerebral, nor merely social or legalistic. To be following the Way, when the Way is a person, means to be coming into fully conscious contact with this person. St Paul talks of union, of being in Christ, of 'putting on Christ'. His language is that of impassioned love rather than cool observance. We can encounter the Jesus who died, because he is the one who also returned from death and this person dwells in the heart of each of us. His human consciousness dwells within ours.

Following the Way is encountering and being true to the consequences of encountering this consciousness. Awakening to the full consciousness of the mind of Christ dwelling in us is something quite different from thinking about Jesus, quite different from thinking about the God he reveals. Awakening to full enlightenment is not the result of thinking or the child of imagination. Awakening to the consciousness of Christ is the enlightenment or the second birth that the gospel calls each person to experience fully. Not to experience it through somebody else's experience by reading, even the Gospel or the great spiritual classics, or by studying any text, directional book or treatises about prayer. But to be a follower of the Way *in* yourself, to be awakening to the Way *for* yourself. Every religious tradition talks of this enlightenment as an awakening. When the Buddha was asked, 'Master, are you the all-wise?' he replied, 'I am the one who is awake.' When Jesus taught his disciples to pray he told them to stay awake. This is the common starting point of all meditation. To awaken to full consciousness through the indwelling mind of Christ means finding Christ as the light itself. He is not only the awakened, but also the awakening power.

There is a real urgency in learning this that we do not get held back from experiencing the truth of it by trying to define what all the words mean. Understanding will only flow fully from actually entering into the experience of union. What it means, to say that the mind of Christ dwells in us, can only be known when we are following the Way and so are awakening to the Way. If we try and extract the meaning from the words separate from the experience of faith we will only be left with more words. This awakening is a journey, a way, a path to fullness of life. The distance between origin and destination is the measure of faith. No one can arrive before they have left. No one can begin without faith. Yet we soon discover that arrival, enlightenment, is not chronological but progressive. The way is a way of realisation, not achievement. When we have fully arrived we will know we have never been anywhere else. Jesus expressed himself as a way and a means by saying, 'I have come that you may have life in all its fullness.' Most of us live a very incomplete life and seek ways to fully develop our humanity. But there is the danger of losing the Way for the ways, missing the wood for the trees, if we are not guided by a tradition and teacher.

Meditation is a way that we follow the Way. It is the way of following it most simply, directly and personally, indeed most ordinarily. The problem we face in trying to follow this radically simple path to become fully awake is twofold. The first is our tendency to fall asleep. Not necessarily physically. That is a hazard of the first stages of meditation because we are not used to being both alert and relaxed and so we tend to doze off when there is nothing immediate and external to do. But there is also the danger of sleeping spiritually, when we go in for a bout of pious dozing, that day-dreaming state of devotional reverie where we are neither awake nor asleep. The greatest enemy of meditation, of the path of awakening, is day-dreaming. The great illusion to avoid is mistaking this state of devotional dozing and religious saturation for pure prayer. We can best avoid that illusion by facing the other great problem, which is the hurdle of distraction.

Beginning to meditate can shock us by disclosing how distracted we really are. A little below the surface of consciousness in our daily mind, we suddenly discover that we are almost totally at the mercy of random thoughts, awash with rampant imaginings, sub-conscious fears, anxieties, memories. We have almost no capacity to concentrate, to pay attention at this level of the teeming mind. We discover just how uncontrolled our over-stimulated imagination is. Everyone discovers this within the first days of meditation, and it is good to discover it as soon as possible. There is no true way that does not take us through these levels of distraction, out into the kingdom of the awakened. It is important to know in advance that we will find ourselves distracted because it is not a pleasant experience.

And it is one that we are often tempted to deny or run away from.

We do not like to feel that we are interiorly in a state of such chaos, and it is far easier to regress into day-dreaming, into pious dozing. Here we face the great discipline and equally great gift of the continual recitation of the mantra. John Main once said that we find God in the place beyond distraction. That 'place' is not anywhere outside us. It is not a question of setting up the ideal environment or finding the perfect community. The place is within us, the heart, for 'the Kingdom of heaven is within you'. To find that place we have to steer a way through uncharted stretches of consciousness where there seem only to be the fogs and storms of distraction. The way through it is the way of meditation. Its purpose is not to explore or chart the great territories of the unconscious but to persevere in singleminded commitment to the goal of pure consciousness, the mind of Christ. Meditation is an ancient way, a tradition that goes back to the teaching of Jesus himself on prayer and is first described in detail by the early monks. The important challenge is not to study the writings of the tradition but to realise how simple and how practical the teaching is. The important question is practical, not why but how? How do we awake to that place beyond distraction, where we find Christ who is the Way to God?

The tradition tells us of it as a way of inner silence, a way of utter simplicity. It is not an easy way, but it is possible for everyone because it is as simple and as childlike as anything that is universally human. The silence does not involve merely keeping quiet by not speaking, singing or muttering, because it is an interior silence. It is important to practise stillness exteriorly, to sit physically still; but the real stillness is again interior. We come to that stillness and silence of mind and heart in a very simple way by repeating a single sacred word or phrase, the mantra, during the entire time of meditation. The only other essential discipline is to meditate for a minimum of two periods a day. This interior and regular fidelity is the kind of commitment that the Way asks of its followers. In this tradition saying the mantra is essentially and for all practical purposes, the way of meditation.

The way of meditation is simple but the act of faith you make in saying the mantra and in meditating twice a day becomes deeper as you proceed. A new depth of consciousness, clearer as it gets deeper, opens up as we make that same act of faith from deeper centres of our personality.

Say the mantra as a sound. It is an almost absurdly simple way, but fidelity to it will lead through distraction to awakening, and to a depth of peace and joy that cannot be imagined because it is beyond all images. As you begin to meditate, in the first weeks or months you will probably ask yourself, 'Why should I follow this particular way? There must be others equally good and less demanding.' We live in an age of multiple choice and there are chains of spiritual supermarkets opening up all around us. New and improved brands are constantly being produced to answer the demand for spiritual teaching. In a consumer mentality there is no right way. There are only more ways. But if we can escape this cultural conditioning and see what meditation is really about we see there is only one Way, the way of poverty of spirit and purity of heart, of compassion and forgiveness; and perseverance is the only way to be true to it. We follow this way of meditation because it leads us on the Way. Our own experience, if we can begin and persevere, teaches each of us that. But we all begin by accepting it on faith. We begin in trust. We begin in faith. We continue in faith.

> The pharisees asked Jesus, 'When will the kingdom of God come?' He said, 'You cannot tell by observation when the kingdom of God comes. There will be no saying, 'Look, here it is!' or 'There it is'; for in fact the kingdom of God is within you. (Luke 17:20–1)

That is why we meditate, to realise that truth.

The Abstraction of Materialism

It takes far less time to explain how to meditate than why one should meditate. In any introductory talk the priority is to explain the 'how' as being more important. We each discover how to express 'why' we should meditate in the process of meditation itself. To begin with this asks for a certain act of faith, a certain leap into the unknown, though not an uninviting one. But it is helpful to have a preliminary understanding about the context in which we are asked to make that act of faith. At least part of the context in which everyone begins is essentially the same for us all because of the society we live in and the effect that living in this society has upon every individual. We are used to thinking of our society as being fanatically materialistic. But we are not inclined to think of ourselves as materialists. No one would like to be called 'materialistic'. Yet we must recognise that in many ways our lifestyle, personality, and habits of mind are conditioned by the excessive concern society shows in profit, productivity and efficiency.

It is, for example, astonishing how few people one meets who are happy in their job. When you ask most people, 'Why are you doing this job that you feel is unworthy of you, unfilling and that you hate so much?' they say 'Well, I have to. I have a right to certain things and I must work to earn them.' A young immigrant worker once virtually told me that his reason for doing a job that was bringing him to the verge of physical and nervous breakdown was the desire for a VCR, the latest consumer status-symbol. He felt he was sovereignly free in working towards that achievement. But in the end his greatest freedom would consist in selecting between a Sony and a Sanyo. A materialistic culture with its compulsive concern with possessions, money, status and success is something we each like to think we stand above. But all the forces of that society mould us. Materialism pursues a policy of subtle and largely subliminal

84

seduction. Perhaps its greatest deception is that it is not materialistic at all. We are used to the platitudes of criticising our materialistic society. Yet the great peril we face is the degree of abstraction that we have reached. The curious curse of a materialistic society is 'abstraction' and the degree to which we consequently live in the head alone, through scientific reason and academic analysis.

What we take to be the purposes of our materialistic quest are not very real or substantial. They are the symbols of the salary we get, the house we live in, the car we drive, the clothes we wear. They are symbols of success and achievement, or of a certain degree of tolerated marginality, symbols of mass-identity. They are abstractions of the material, and so they fail to satisfy the material desires they represent. Only solid reality, where mind and matter are integrated can fully satisfy. Without such integration, even as we achieve these symbols, we find that discontent and anxiety mount. They are images, not actuality, photographic not personal reality. The same process of abstraction occurs in the way we relate to our personhood, not just in the social jobs and roles of parents, spouses, friends or teachers, but in the way we know our selves interiorily. Wherever there is abstraction there is also alienation. When we abstract and dematerialise something we alienate ourselves from it. We objectify it and look *at it* out there. We rupture the delicate thread that unites all external reality to the interior universe of consciousness. Empathy and compassion, as well as the awareness of our being an integral part of creation, depend upon this subtle union of consciousness and matter.

It is of the very essence of being human that we are committed to a search for our inner selves in a world where we feel at home. Life is then a developing and expansive process. We are indeed all searching for our selves. However absorbed we may seem to be in our myopic materialism we are searching out the true, long-range identity of ourselves, and we know that the search will only be concluded if we find the source of creation. In modern society with its mighty powers of abstraction, a psychological form of spirituality has become a major industry. Methods, games or techniques of self-knowledge, self-realisation, self-fulfilment or self-discovery are, however, often a futile search that leads no further than more images of self. The more cerebral and abstract it becomes, the more it leads to a worse sense of alienation. Even the physical methods of this industry are cerebrally controlled and lead to imbalance. It is bad enough to be alienated from society, from the environment and from the people with whom we live. But when we are alienated from ourselves, we have a major crisis. The natural powers of self-regeneration are weakened. What we find in the materialistic search for our true selves is frequently only an abstraction of the self, an image of a distant reality, some one else's ideology.

Much of the modern search for selfhood and identity is conducted with the aid of systems. Complex intellectual systems expressing cerebral or psychological patterns are often simplified, packaged and popularised. They are organised around a structure of types of personalities. When we apply this system to ourselves or have somebody else apply it to us, usually at a certain cost, we find ourselves being sorted and categorised. At the end of the process we may feel, and are meant to feel, a momentary thrill of self-discovery. We have a label by which the system tells us what number or type we are or what unique combination of types we belong to. But it is a short-lived experience. The letters or numbers that inform us of what we are, soon begin to fade in their power to tell us *who* we are and so to overcome the critical sense of self-alienation. Materialistic spirituality offers a self-knowledge that is soon exposed as spurious, shallow, or even another kind of self-deception.

Meditation is a spiritual path. It is not a materialistic system. It is not concerned with profit, productivity, efficiency or definability. It is not a cerebral system because it does not work by analysis or comparison. But it is a path. Meditation is a way to what the human being as a whole is searching for. The conviction that it is the simplest, the humblest and truest, and most direct path to what we are all searching for becomes the reason why we persevere. Because it is a path to true selfhood it overcomes self-alienation. It is synonymously a path to God.

Self-knowledge and experience of God unfold together and into each other. It is vital, if we have any spiritual vision of life, to be on such a path that is a true way of self-knowledge, because only that way will lead to God. It is a path in which we leave egoism or incomplete selfhood behind, the egoism that tries to control and monitor the process of self-knowledge. Egotistical consciousness is that frame of mind where we revere ourselves as the objective centre of reality. As we meditate, we discover the truth that we are not reality's centre. We leave the illusory and painful state of egoism behind as we pass through the ordeals of growth into the joy of full being.

How do we make this transition from self-centred and self-conscious egoism, into full being and true selfhood? Very simply, is the answer. Very silent. Very still. Stillness brings us to the awareness of wholeness, the integration of body and mind in spirit. It is not a path for analysing ideas, feelings or anxieties. Of course we sit down to meditate each morning and evening with our share of the world's problems, our own complex feelings, but these are not the times to be pondering, solving or reviewing them. Let go of your anxieties is the advice of Jesus as teacher of prayer. That sounds easy. But it is utterly simple. And so it is possible, if we can trust it. Anything so simple is possible if we are faithful to it. So do not work on your agenda, do not balance the books of your life. Say your mantra. If you find, as you inevitably will, that you get distracted, simply, humbly (it is a very humbling and ordinary process) return to it. Come back to the mantra whenever you realise that you have stopped saying it.

It is not a time for dreaming. If you find yourself going off into a nice day-dream, come back to reality through the mantra. If you find yourself probing your nightmares, come back from your fears through the mantra. It is not even a time for thinking. If you find yourself thinking about why you are saying the mantra, exit from the labyrinth of thought with the mantra. Meditation is a way of inner silence and a discipline of wakefulness. What is attractive about it as a path is also what is challenging about it. This is the experience of solitude.

It is important, if we want to understand why we are meditating, to see the distinction between solitude and loneliness. Solitude is the conscious, accepting awareness of our uniqueness. It has nothing to do with isolation. Solitude is to know who we are uniquely; whereas loneliness is the fearful suppression of that uniqueness through surrender to the impersonal, collective forces of uniformity, and standardisation. We are gripped by such an epidemic of loneliness in our society because there is so much impersonal standardisation, such forces of conformity. We assess ourselves and others so much by types, categories and labels. Categorisation suppresses the uniqueness of selfhood and creates alienation and loneliness.

The cure for this epidemic is the experience of solitude contained in what has traditionally been called the 'contemplative experience' or 'pure prayer'. It is a radical cure and a demanding treatment. But it is a joy to discover and a joy to follow. Those times of meditation each day, root us progressively deeper in the true self. The fruit of meditation is not to be assessed by anything that happens during the meditation. Ignore anything that happens, but be prepared for your life to be changed. The sign that your life is being changed will come through your life's network of relationships. We are not just recharging our batteries when we meditate. We are making a journey, undergoing a transformation. The growth is the journey towards the vision of God in ourself and in others. And, in the Christian understanding, it is empowered by the vision of the true self of God revealed in Christ.

> May the God of peace . . . make you perfect in all goodness so that you may do his will; and may he make of us what he would have us be through Jesus Christ, to whom be glory for ever and ever.   (Heb. 13:20)

That is why we meditate – so that we may be made who God would have us be – our true self.

The Joy of Disillusionment

Doctors and nurses often comment on the difficulty they face in trying to diagnose a child's illness. A child will come in looking evidently distressed and the doctor asks what is the matter. The child says it hurts. The doctor asks where and the child replies, 'I don't know.' The diagnosis proceeds with great difficulty when the patient cannot locate the source or describe the nature of the pain. Adults are not that different when it comes to their awareness of the cause and nature of their psychological or spiritual suffering. The anxiety or the depression that are prevalent characteristics of our lifestyle are felt keenly enough but far more rarely understood. 'I don't know why I feel so miserable, or restless or fearful!'

Faced with that kind of pain or discontent we usually conclude that something important is lacking in our life; something has gone wrong; I have forgotten something I once knew; I am looking for something, but I don't know whether it was lost or is anticipated. It is often felt that if it hurts, it is because life was running ahead too fast without looking where it was going and ran off the road at a sharp corner of reality. It is reality that hurts. Life hurts. This explanation gives rise to the widespread belief, epidemic in our culture today, that reality is less attractive than fantasy. Life as it is, reality as it is, is second best because we can all imagine something better. Everyone can fantasise about what would make them fulfilled, happy and satisfied and recognises where 'reality' falls short of the 'ideal'.

Once we have been caught by this insidious belief, that reality is not as good as we could make it, we spend more and more time and human and material resources playing games, constructing fantasy. Reality-as-I-would-like-it-to-be becomes a major consumer of time as well as a growth-industry. If this belief becomes sufficiently widespread and enough people get caught in it – it is very persuasive – then a whole society, personal lifestyles, and whole lifetimes can be based on working hard in order to support fantasy, to pay for the dream holiday, buy the perfect house, look and smell like the gods and goddesses of the screen. Because of the kind of self-determining society we live in, everyone is to some degree caught in the net of alternative realities. No one is unaffected by it. Its very intrusiveness leads to an intensification of the anxiety and the depression which we were trying to escape. It leads to the recurrent nightmare that this fantasy game could take us over completely because, thinking that we are the players, we eventually become trapped and absorbed by the game we started. This gives rise in no small degree to the deep and unsettling, often vague fear that people throughout the world are feeling.

We should know that we all have a frightening capacity for self-deception. A recent book on Mr Reagan's presidency describes how some years ago he was giving a speech during a visit of the Japanese prime minister to the United States. The President described in very moving terms his visit to a concentration camp at the end of the war. It was such a visual and moving description that both the President and the Japanese prime minister repeated it in the course of the visit. But it was later discovered that it was a completely untrue story and the White House admitted that he had never personally visited the camps but had read reports by those who had liberated them. The author of the book suggests that this was an example of sincere self-deception. This is what the President felt should have happened and it would be better if it had happened and, therefore, he could easily make-believe that it did happen. We feel we can make reality happen. Not all of us are quite so sincerely capable of his kind of self-deception. But we all try.

And what we cannot do for ourselves we allow the media, politicians, or the entertainment industry to do for us. The two great forces that compete for control of consciousness are reality and illusion. We tend to prefer illusion, in what we think of as safe doses, because reality seems to hurt. But what actually hurts, when you diagnose the suffering, is disappointment. When hopes are disappointed the pain of dis-illusionment spreads throughout the system. When we blame reality it is a sign of how deeply we are caught in the net of illusion and the stratagems by which illusion protects itself. Illusion is like a terrorist, backed up by the secret super-power of the ego. It may constantly be defeated but it always comes back with new resources.

The basic fallacy in the network of illusion can be traced back and laid at the feet of the ego. The ego is that fiercely defended sense of separateness, of proud specialness and vain uniqueness. It is this sense that spins the most controlling web-fantasy of all, which is the illusion that we are the centre of reality. This is the last and most strongly guarded illusion to be shattered. The truth is that we *are* special and unique. The problem arises in that we are not special or unique where we think we are. What we may think is unique about us is not. It is more often a part of us that is collective and that makes us part of the crowd.

The crowd is merely the great, pre-personal collective ego. What we frequently think of as inaccessible and part of a common human nature, and vaguely call a soul, is what is, in fact, the true, unique identity of our personhood, our Self. Separating the two forces of reality and illusion reveals the uniqueness of each personal Self as it shares in a common human nature. It is the work of enlightenment, the supremely human work to reveal and liberate it. Nothing else in creation, apart from the human being, is enlightened because nothing else is self-deceived. Enlightenment is a process of increasingly refined discrimination that proceeds through a series of disillusionments. Many disillusionments. The process of enlightenment, of coming into reality, and so of being realised, involves a replaying of the tape of experience, an exodus from daily life and a going back. The result of this dynamic of prayer is a diagnosis and cure of all illusions and self-deceptions until we eventually get back to that primary, infantile illusion that we are God, and the centre of the world. Shedding illusions, which involves a certain uncovering of repression and some hard self-knowledge, becomes harder as we approach the fundamental constructions of fantasy, the origin of sin. But each disillusionment is a victory that boosts morale for the next stage. The journey into reality that is the process of disillusionment is the way of meditation. As you learn to meditate, on a daily basis, you run a thread of reality through your life to draw it into unity and to activate the process of enlightenment in every dimension. If you are faithful to the discipline, the process unfolds with a steady, unstoppable momentum.

To sit down to meditate is to give oneself wholeheartedly to reality. The way of meditation is a way of allowing reality to be and so of being freed in spirit by finding that it is not we who are the centre of reality but reality that is at the centre of us. Lacking in difficult theories or esoteric knowledge or practices, meditation presents us with only one major problem, caught in the web of illusion as we are. It is *simple*. The more implicated we get in illusion, the more complex we become. Simplicity is difficult to accept when the mind is ruled by reflexive complexity. There is another problem. Meditation is a *discipline*, that is, not something to play around with. It is something that asks, not a solemn or self-important commitment, but one that is truly serious. It is a commitment to reality that grows in time, with the practice of the humility of the mantra. Life is from beginning to end a learning process. We are learning in the school of reality and the first lesson is to learn how to meditate.

Meditation does not achieve reality by thought. You are not thinking when you meditate. You are being. The thoughts will involuntarily come and you let them freely go. Do not pay attention to any idea or image. They will come and they will go. But the mantra stays constant. Everything else at the time is distraction. Say the mantra, listen to the mantra, give of yourself *through* the mantra. We need to meditate each day because the illusions in which we get caught are constantly re-forming, and meditation releases the power of reality that constantly dissolves them. It takes us out of the grip of fantasy and fear by uncovering the power of reality in the divine love within us.

The teaching of Jesus is that reality is already within us and *of* us. When we can believe him, we are free of illusion. The Spirit of Christ teaches us from within as we allow ourselves to be teachable. Meditation is simply a response in faith to the call of Jesus to find the Kingdom of reality within us. This reality is described in the New Testament in many ways, as Kingdom, Truth, Life. It is described by St John and by St Peter as like light, a light that is shining in the dark place of unreality, radiant and redemptive in the midst of illusion. As we give our attention to this reality, it expands. It grows and illuminates the darkness, dissolves the illusion.

All this only confirms for us the message of the prophets, to which you will do well to attend, because it is like a lamp shining in a murky place, until the day breaks and the morning star rises to illuminate your minds.   (2 Pet. 1:19)

The Use of Detail

Every artist knows that if you want to achieve a likeness of what you want to represent or to articulate your impressions, you have to be wholly attentive to detail. You have to select the right details and present them in the right way. The same is true of every attempt to communicate. You have to edit experience if you want to communicate anything of importance to others. Clarity and empathy do not result from a bombardment but from a discrimination of detail. What economy is to the artist, poverty is to the meditator.

If the right detail is captured in the right way and set in the right perspective, awareness is heightened. But more often than not the details are out of our control. In their multiplicity they swamp us. We are overpowered by the endlessness of detail. Like flies they come at us from every angle. They pile up in the wrong places, they obsess us. We often become slowly obsessive or compulsive about trivia that can loom so large that they defocus clarity and disturb our peace. We may well know that this is happening. We may see that a detail of life, a situation or emotion, has got out of proportion but somehow it cannot be pushed back into its right place. The result of involuntary selection of detail, what we generally call obsession, is not clarity but confusion, not communication but isolation. When the details get out of control and swamp us, the confusion that is created is a major cause of suffering because when we are confused we do everything wrong. Mistakes are made in the most simple things, in the most ordinary relationships as well as the most important relationships. The bus driver scowls. The wife nags. The husband retreats. Mistakes happen in the routine things that we know how to do perfectly well. We make misperceptions, misjudgements and somehow know that they are mistaken and yet cannot extricate the particular from the general confusion. And if confusion is allowed to tighten its hold it can destroy the perception of reality altogether as neurosis slips into psychosis. When peace has gone we lose the essential sense of being involved with reality and become observers of life rather than people who are living. Modern information systems, new communication networks and the constant stimulation of the imaginative needs of people, have flooded contemporary life with detail. People complain incessantly of pressure and confusion.

To compensate for the confusion which arises in the emotions and the intellect, in relationships and organisations, it is a tempting option to create an alternative version of reality. We simulate clarity and impose a false grid of meaning over the chaos of feeling and event. But of course we do not have that power to create reality. As the artist knows, the highest creative power is to reflect and reverence reality. We cannot control reality to suit us without creating the mirror-image we know as the seductive but destructive force of fantasy. Illusion employed as the basis of action inevitably leads to conflict within ourselves, and so between ourselves and others.

The starting point for anyone beginning to meditate, with whatever degree of faith, is to accept that we are confused. We have all experienced the confusion that results from the disappointed false hopes proffered by illusion, more or less intensely at different times. At whatever stage of the journey to reality we may be when we begin to meditate, we begin confused. To be confused means to be mistaken, and the anxiety that is created by this inaccuracy – this missing of the mark, or sin – leads to a labyrinth of error: disappointments, disharmonies, anger, depression, misunderstanding, insecurity. We begin to meditate and persevere in the daily discipline because the deepest human longing, our deepest need and summons is to find peace and clarity.

At work or with the family or in any relationship, a situation becomes clouded. There is a moment to say, 'Let's sit down and try and talk this through, let's try and get to the heart of our problem.' What that means, in fact, when it is human beings involved, is that we must get to the heart of the people concerned. It is not events or life that is confused. It is people who are confused. *We* are dis-ordered, and so the heart of the problem is always the human heart. The great problem is not will *they* open their hearts, but will *we* open our hearts, to release the clarifying power of love?

In the heart clarity and peace are present in potential. Meditation takes us directly, not easily or by any shortcut but absolutely, simply, to the centre of all reality and contacts the power that realises all potential. When we meditate we come to the personal centre of being which the Bible calls the heart and, as we do so, the truth dawns that the personal heart is the place of God. Every person is the one and unique centre of God, every heart the threshold of all reality. It is the doorway to the inner life of God (in as much as it makes sense to talk of inner and outer about God), when all propositions – with, in and through – are equally and simultaneously true. To begin to meditate is to accept a knowledge that we may try to wriggle out of but eventually must bow to, that the core of every problem is the confusion in our own heart. The clarity and peace we seek is to be found there and nowhere else.

We discover some clarity as soon as we accept that self-knowledge and stop blaming others, God, the economy or fate. On the journey to the centre, the self-knowledge of realism, called humility, arises. We see things clearly and to see clearly is to experience beauty, and in the contemplation of beauty the energy of peace restores harmony. Beauty is in the heart of the beholder. That is why meditation opens up the capacity to see beauty. But there is more involved than meditating once or twice to enjoy the experience at random. This would be to treat meditation as an aesthetic activity, like a visit to a gallery or a concert. Meditation makes artists of us all, practitioners not observers. Yet it is even more demanding than art because not only the selection of detail but the renunciation of all detail is asked for: poverty. It is a matter of persevering in this renunciation. Neither renunciation nor perseverance is ever perfect. There is a constant intrusion of detail, the involuntary surrender to the mind's struggle to achieve its own control over experience. We learn how to persevere by learning to begin again and again, and to understand that meditation is itself a learning process. It is learning to believe that we see things clearly by unlearning the confused habits of thought, feeling and perception that the errors of illusion have imposed. Meditation is learning to unlearn the engrained responses we wrongly think of as our real nature. Every time we sit down to meditate we take another first step in this process. If we always see ourselves as beginners there is no reason that all of us should not complete this increasingly wonderful and joyful journey to peace and clarity in the divine love that burns in the centre of our being.

When we first begin to meditate we discover to our shame just how confused a state prevails. The first and longest lasting symptom of confusion is distraction. Do not be unduly surprised or at all discouraged by the degree of distraction you encounter. Because the inner world is in constant touch with external events as well as having its own agenda, the level of distraction will fluctuate. Nothing would be more detrimental to progress than to assess your progress by the current level of distraction. If you feel you have had a totally useless meditation because of the high level of distraction you may never be more wrong. If you do not ever have any distraction it would be fair to suspect you are not really meditating. More likely you are just sinking into the distractions and confusion or just falling asleep. Similarly, when people say that they find the mantra itself a distraction they have made a basic confusion between clarity and capitulation, peace and comfort. Distractions are no indication that meditation is not for you. They are every indication that you should persevere.

Modern culture with its speed-of-light communication, its bombardment of the collective consciousness with charged detail, its media-flood of trivia from the time you turn on in the morning to the time you turn off at night, has made the human mind more distracted, more confused than at any other period in history. Under all these pressures it is not surprising that when we begin to meditate the mind is racing. It is as if it is a merry-go-round, a carousel of revolving shapes and sounds. What distinguishes distraction from the creative imagination is precisely the obsessional, cyclical nature of its processes and contents. The same things keep on coming up, the same details, anxieties and problems. It takes time to slow that down but, as it slows down, the blur begins to resolve. And our perception of reality, as well as our involvement with real as opposed to imaginative life, advances in clarity and focus. The change from being confused to being focused happens through fidelity to the mantra. Learning to say the mantra – and the mantra is the great test of how seriously we want to be clear – is the discipline of humility and of patience. But it is also the constant verification of the journey into reality. We know we are making the journey because we are committed to the mantra. That awareness in itself begins to turn the mind from confusion to clarity. To know that a beginning has been made is to know that a way exists and that a focus is being established. To know we are committed to growth, is the beginning of growth.

The mantra will become more rooted, more constant. Saying the mantra inevitably creates some resistance in us through the ego, which is the source of confusion throughout the process of spiritual evolution. One of the ways it will try to persuade us to give up is the familiar materialistic voice: 'What am I getting out of this? What is all this producing? Is my investment justified by its returns? Why should I bother to go for clarity?' It is all-important to persevere, if only in 'sheer faith', until you begin to taste the clarity and to experience that energy of peace, because then you will know for yourself that it does not have to be justified by any materialistic standards. Clarity is simply what we are created for and all good things flow from it. To see God with a pure, unclouded heart is to know reality, to be open to the beauty of God in every one of his self-showings.

> Then he showed me the river of the water of life, sparkling like crystal, flowing from the throne of God and of the Lamb down the middle of the city's street . . . Come forward, you who are thirsty; accept the water of life, a free gift to all who desire it.   (Rev. 22:1, 17)

The clear water of the Spirit is within our own hearts and it is freely given. It is only necessary to learn to open our heart to release it and so to be purified by it. It is the mantra, and our fidelity, humility and good will in learning to say it, that opens the heart to the clarifying light.

The Success of Failure

Thomas Edison used to conduct an average of five thousand experiments on every one of his projects. It is said that each time one of these experiments failed he would smile and be happy that he had found another way the invention could not work. He knew he had come a little closer to discovering the right way.

We live in a society which makes us believe that only success counts and that failure is shameful, something we do not willingly acknowledge or speak about except perhaps to those closest to us. Failure makes us look absurd. Failure is a waste of time. Failure humiliates us. With the kind of conditioning that education and business reinforce, we tend to hide our failures and to pretend to be successful. This obsession with success and fear of failure, so different from Thomas Edison's truly creative outlook where success and failure were twin-parts of the same process of discovery, has come to dominate every area of activity. Not just careers and sport and financial and social status, but emotional and intellectual life are also seen competitively. We need to be a success at everything, and failure in anything can severely shake our self-respect and sense of identity. Mastery, excellence and success compose the prevalent social image that people are expected to aspire to and then maintain because, when we slip, it is not certain where we will stop falling. Yet the truth is that all human beings are only too well acquainted with failure. Everyone fails far more often than they succeed. And indeed when we do succeed we often find it has been in something we did not really intend to do. Everyone who has 'made it' knows that large degrees of chance and the unconscious must be added to talent and drive.

When life is seen in these narrow socially conditioned terms of success and failure, we find ourselves alienated from the real achievements that make meaning and convey value. Those achievements occur when we are not competitively trying to succeed but are giving ourselves to the work in hand generously and without concern for the final evaluation. Those achievements of true commitment are the ones that form and constitute us for eternity. They are the only things that really matter. And they rarely directly concern our economic or social standing. If we find ourselves living primarily for success and denying or repressing failure then we will find that we have lost contact with our true self, our real identity. A one-sided concern with success involves living on the surface of life, out of touch with the depth-dimension, often only discovered through failure, that gives a horizon of meaning to all events. Alternating between death and resurrection, shade and light, failure and success, life is a progressive discovery of who and why we are, how we are connected with a larger meaning, a pattern beyond and yet including ourselves. If we are only success-oriented, we will inevitably misread the pattern and distort the meaning by placing ourselves at its centre and we will be isolated from those depths in ourselves from which comes the energy of growth. The success-fixation results from placing the egotistical, acquisitive and possessive drive at the centre of life, to which it tends to be attracted even against our better will. The problem for modern people is that we do not have easy access to those sources of wisdom in the spiritual tradition that teach us how to resist that tendency to succumb to ego-centredness.

In fact, we are all exposed and prone to forces in the world that re-enforce the ego as being the ultimate centre of reality because it is the usual centre of human life. We are told by teachers and advertisers to be ego-centred. It is vital for our survival, not only personally but also as a society, to get back in touch with a wisdom that reveals the true centre. Because we are so indoctrinated to act as if the ego is the source of meaning, we often live an ego-centred life without fully understanding it. So much so, that we bring this ego-centred concern with success right into the spiritual life. In turning to the spiritual area of life we automatically start looking for success just as we do in the financial, intellectual or social areas. In coming to pray we expect to succeed all the easier because there seems no one else to compete with. This is where spirituality becomes self-indulgent, introverted and escapist. The paradox is that to succeed in prayer means to accept the failure and unconditional surrender of the ego. If we are trying to succeed in any other way we are locked in the absurdity of the ego trying to cast out itself.

This is why it is so vital to ensure that at the pivotal point of the spiritual life we are aware of being committed to the transcendence of the ego. Not to accommodating the ego, but to a simple and ultimate transcendence of the ego. This may involve a long process with many phases, one of which may be the repair of a damaged psyche. But the commitment to transcendence is the essential stimulus to growth and healing. We do not in fact ever achieve success in the spiritual life. Success itself is an ego-concept.

Think of that concept of success. What does it mean? It means *my* goals, *my* efforts, and *my* rewards. But if we are following a spiritual path (and there is no life that is balanced or meaningful unless we are), we discover something infinitely more satisfying than success perceived as the achievement of imaginatively conceived desires. We discover instead the realisation of the unimaginable, which is the coming into reality of who we are. Meditation is a spiritual path and it is a selfless path of self-realisation. It is not useful to think of it only as a path of *self*-realisation. But approach it as a path of selfless-realisation, and success and failure do not need to enter into it at all. Once it is truly being followed as a spiritual path with the commitment to transcendence, the Christian experience of discipleship dawns and with it liberation and joy. From deep within, the meditator begins to taste the expansive and sustained freedom that success can never give.

On the first occasion you meditate, you will experience failure. If, that is, you are trying to succeed. It can only be failure if there was an attempt to succeed. To some extent we are all trying to succeed at first, because the ego colours everything we do. But it is important to recognise that the feeling of failure, which you may have not only today but in ten years' time as well, is sheer illusion. It is simply to be ignored. Experience, practice and fidelity to the mantra will give you the strength of consciousness to dismiss that idea of failure as soon as it intrudes itself and begins to discourage you.

What is it, though, we feel we have failed in? It seems immediately to be the failure to concentrate, to be still, to say the mantra. Absurdly we fail to follow the way of total simplicity. That tells us a great deal about meditation. Meditation is utterly simple. And if we fail to meditate it is because we are not yet simple enough. We are still too complicated by egoism. But the regular practice of meditation steadily reduces the complexity of the ego and simplifies us. And so meditation is its own success. To succeed in meditation, simply persevere in it. That is the utterly simple joy of it. The way of meditation is really as simple as it sounds, however hard it may be for us to be reconciled to that simplicity.

You repeat the mantra from the beginning to the end of the meditation, or you try to. And trying to, you find that you fail countless times because of silly distractions, recurrent anxieties, daily problems and natural restlessness, because we watch too much television, because we have too many expectations of what should happen. But every time you realise that you have stopped saying the word, very simply, very gently and faithfully come back to it and start saying it again, silently and interiorly. The only thing that should discourage you is if you think that you have succeeded! That is a serious problem to solve, to think you are a spiritual success. But persevering in meditation will change all the perspectives of your outlook. Firstly, on meditation itself and next on the values of life as a whole. A discovery awaits, through the experience of depth, of a new way of perceiving yourself and the successes and failures of ordinary life. A deeper meaning, that is of more resonance and radiance than anything hitherto suspected, begins to be felt. As we persevere we become gradually realised, gradually enlightened, gradually free. We become more loving because the great power released in us as we become simple is the power of love. And so, we say the mantra, not more successfully, but more faithfully.

Meditation always humbles us. Failure, however, often humiliates us. It crushes pride but can also lead to shame and self-rejection. But this is not the nature of humility. True humility is the condition of wisdom. It leads to the understanding that, though we do indeed make mistakes, God cannot. If we think self-rejectingly of ourselves as ultimate failures then we cannot believe in God, because God has not failed with us. As we realise who we are, we come to realise who God is. Meditation leads us to know God, the Creator and the Ground of our being. It simultaneously leads to the realisation of who

Christ is. We see him as the fully realised one who has broken the dualism of success and failure and transcended the ego through his death and resurrection. The light of his loving self shines in each of us.

Saying the mantra is a very humble and simple work. It is joyful work but it is also discipline. Meditation is the daily labour that earns the daily bread of being changed by the powers of the Kingdom. It is a simple work in which we are totally detached from the fruit of our labour or the expectation of reward, but which transforms our life. Saying the mantra is the work of meditation and it is the way to realisation beyond the confines of egoism, self-interest and success.

All of this is understood in the mind of Christ which, St Peter says, rises in us to enlighten our mind:

> All this only confirms for us the message of the prophets, to which you will do well to attend, because it is like a lamp shining in a murky place, until the day breaks and the morning star rises to illuminate your minds.   (2 Pet. 1:19)

Here is the illumination of the way of meditation.

The Cycle of Love

One of the many fascinating things you discover about meditation when trying to communicate it to others is that its essential idea is extremely attractive to people. However, explaining what this essential idea is, is less easy. One could say it consists in the understanding of the existence in each person of a truthful, real and loving self-identity. Even if this self is not known to the person or to his or her closest intimates, its existence is intuited. And although referring to it sometimes incurs an aggressive defence reaction, in general meditation gently affirms its existence and potential.

Meditation seems to evoke a deep response while at the same time being a disturbing teaching to hear. As modern people we are subjects of experience, which means that we want to know for ourselves and to be able to verify every claim in our own experience. No doubt this is partly why meditation is generally attractive, because it is purely experiential. It is personal, it asks for a wholehearted engagement, and it is direct, dispensing with all forms of mediation. It does not matter how many books you read on it or how many talks you hear about it. When meditation is seriously undertaken it is you who have to do it, because it is your experience. In time we come to realise that a purely personal experience is also always relational to others. But, at first, it is deeply attractive because it is rightly felt that personal experience is integral to the way of truth. Yet, it is as challenging as it is attractive. It challenges because of the type of personal experience that meditation invites and involves. John Main opened the way to understand this aspect of meditation by saying that when you meditate do not try to experience-the-experience. When we meditate we enter the experience-in-itself. As modern self-reflective people, interested in the varieties of experience, we are preconditioned to be more interested in experiencing the experience. We want

104

to be able to remember it, write about it, talk about it, compare and communicate it.

But at the time of meditation itself we are un-learning that self-conscious, ego-controlled approach. There is neither ana-lysing of the experience, nor trying to save the experience. There is only learning, no doubt slowly but no less directly, to allow what is to be itself. Whatever happens, say the mantra. Say it until you can no longer say it. And as soon as you realise you have stopped saying it, start saying it again. Here is a formula, utterly simple, utterly practical, that can lead any sincere and serious person into the experience-in-itself which is the experience of being, the knowledge of God. As modern people we may find that refreshingly and attractively simple, but we immediately try to find a way around it. One of the easiest ways to avoid the demand of such simplicity is to say in an emphatically moderate and sweetly reasonable tone of voice, 'Well, of course, say the mantra, but don't say it the whole time. Just say it until it leads you to an experience and when you are there relax into it and enjoy the experience.' But Christian prayer is about more than relaxation. It is about peace, a state of divinising energy, not of recharging mental batteries. It is about more than sharpening our self-conscious awareness; it is about knowing the mind of Christ.

What is so challenging about meditation is the way it leads us to the experience of non-experience. This is what poverty of spirit is about. We always want to know what is happening. We want to know what is going to happen. We want to know what happened. Such desire for knowledge is intrinsically pos-sessive. But if we are truly committed to the pilgrimage of personhood and so truly disciples of the Spirit we are not acquiring experience or seeking enrichment from it. We are entering the experience of non-experience, that poverty of spirit where we enjoy everything by possessing nothing.

The wonderful discovery to be made by beginning to follow this way of faith is that the experience of non-experience is the most important experience of all. It is like the basic starting programme that allows a computer to start functioning. Sim-plicity is what the pilgrim is looking for, and it is the richest and ultimately fulfilling experience of life. Gradually, as we allow ourselves to be encouraged and taught, and as we become more faithful, we find in this experience of non-experience, where nothing seems to be happening, that in fact something very real *is* happening. But this simple encounter with reality, which is the motive power of growth, is not in our control. It is gift. It is spirit. As gift or, as the elders call it, grace, it leads to an ever-deeper poverty, a freer letting go. This is what meditators are engaged upon. It is the journey we are all making. But how can we understand it? It *is* necessary to understand it because at every step on the journey we are called to deeper commitment, and I think we can only commit ourselves more deeply if we understand more fully, so that a fuller awareness of what we are doing carries us forward to do it more wholeheartedly.

One of the ways in which we can understand it is the way in which John Main linked meditation to the Gospel's conversion of heart and to the essential process of growth through transcendence. The most important way we can understand the experience of non-experience is by how it takes us into the heart of Christian theology, the central Christian insight into meaning. We can only understand the journey of prayer fully by the analogy of human love.

One of the most common human conditions and perhaps the greatest cause of suffering is the sense of being unloved. We can feel that we are not loved, or not valued for being who we are, for several reasons: because our love for another is not returned, because we feel essentially unlovable, unworthy or emotionally inadequate. Whether it is because we remain unaware of our true worth or because we love without a complementary response, the sense of not being loved causes our deepest suffering. It makes it necessary for us to live each day coping with a deep-seated and mounting sense of non-being. Because if we feel unloved we fear non-entity. Learning to live at more than a coping, survival level involves discovering how we can respond to that feeling of love-longing and respond to it not by evasion, distraction or by numbing ourselves, but by truly facing it and dealing with it. How does the teaching tell us to respond to it?

The Gospel says respond with fidelity and turn around. Face the other direction. 'Keep loving' the gospels say, just as the teaching on meditation says, 'Keep saying your mantra.' If you remain faithful in the middle of this pain, if you keep turning outwards despite feeling unloved, then you will grow beyond that feeling and the pain of loss or absence will become the pain of growth. The sense of unworthiness or inadequacy will give way to a more real self-knowledge of godlikeness. And the pain of unrequited love will acquire a sacrificial dignity. But how do we grow? How do we keep turning in the right direction? If love does not complete its circuit and remains unearthed, if it does not become reciprocal, it must return to its sender. But then it pushes deeper down into the heart from which it emerges. It continues to press down deeper and deeper until it reaches its own source. As it pushes its way back, seeking its own origin, love leads us forward on the path of self-knowledge and self-discovery. It leads to the path contained within that way, the path of self-transcendence. So our love becomes less and less egotistical the more deeply it pushes back and acquires stronger and purer intensity.

With fidelity to the conversion process initiated by the mantra, we begin to be grasped by one of the great mysteries of meditation, which is also its true test. It is that by meditating faithfully we become more loving. But it is a journey, and many times it will give only the sense of swimming against the current of self-rejection, of despair or compromise. In prayer there is a continual pushing back towards our own source until the love that wants to reach out to the world, reaches its own source, in the centre of our being. There we discover that our very capacity and longing to love is a gift from God. However inadequate, unworthy or unloved we may feel henceforth, we can never despair. Because in knowing that the love we feel and long to communicate is a divine quality, we know that everything we are and feel is known and contained by the love of God. This sign that we are loved by God gradually proves that we are loved infinitely. When our love has reached its own source it is reintegrated with itself and becomes capable of selfless expression and fidelity. This is the redemptive experience. Without it, Christianity is just an idea, or just a religion. Meditation reveals Christianity as more than an ideology or a religion but as an imitation of and participation in the divine nature. Christ is just another name while we lack the experience that the source of human love is God in the human heart. We are made whole, we are made wholly loving by discovering this. We love now with a new power that flows from a personal certainty of being loved. Only then are we able to communicate the redemptive experience to others, because we know what redemption is and are not embarrassed to share that knowledge that erases all fear of rejection. Free to love, free to be who we are meant to be, we find that the mantra has led us home and home is where we start from each day.

The wonder of the discovery of love at our own source is that this accelerating momentum of love is contained within our humanity, within its mortality and within all the limitations of body and mind and psyche. Despite frailty, our inconsistency, doubt and all our lapses, this power of love is faithful to us. The more we travel back into it, the more we are able to communicate it and find the fulfilment of the mystery of love in the completed cycle. Demanding always to be completed, straining always to be given, received and returned, the tripartite dynamic of love propels us beyond the sad duality of egoism and its incapacity for transcendence into *the third*, the other. As our experience of love works its transforming power it begins to make ultimate sense to say that whoever loves, lives in God and is being conformed to the nature of the divine.

> The same God who said, 'Out of darkness let light shine', has caused his light to shine within us, to give the light of revelation – the revelation of the glory of God in the face of Jesus Christ. We are no better than pots of earthenware to contain this treasure, and this proves that such transcendent power does not come from us, but is God's alone. (2 Cor. 4:6–8)

The Face of Christ

Leonardo da Vinci's 'Last Supper' is one of the world's great paintings. Leonardo himself is one of the few great geniuses who exemplify how many dimensions human consciousness possesses. In him, as in a very few people, so many of those dimensions are brought to their highest development. But if you look closely at the face of Christ, the central figure in that painting, you will see that it is unfinished. One of the most curious features of Leonard's personality is that, unlike Michelangelo who was deeply concerned about his life's work, his opus, his legacy and place in history, Leonardo seemed sublimely unconcerned with his reputation. What he left behind to go into the textbooks did not preoccupy him. And so one of the paradoxical aspects of his lifelong search for wholeness and completeness is that he left so many things in his life incomplete. It is, I think, part of his greatness that he was able to accept the inevitable incompleteness of life.

We all know this incompleteness in our own experience. We sense it whenever we say to ourselves, 'Why has this happened?' A sense of mystery, or of something inexplicable suggests something unfinished. It is as if it does not quite fit into the pattern or the symmetry that we had wanted to impose on life to force an end. There are always loose ends and we cannot really continue the work of entering the wholeness of life, which is coming to our *own* wholeness, if we become obsessed with stray details. But our conditioned mentality, the way we are trained through the reinforcement of the ego, urges us to cover up the incompleteness. One of the ways we do this is to repress the stray details, but there are other ways in which we do it. Projection of our feelings on to others or pretending to be something or someone that we are not in order to win others' approval are also ways in which we simulate completeness.

We are trained and urged to do a kind of cosmetic job on

life so as to make it seem more whole than it is, or than it can be as yet. Part of the reason behind this conditioning, so strong in our ego-centred culture where the image of self is the operating principle in so much of education, is that incompleteness represents failure. And failure is very hurtful to the ego. The ego is always trying to cover up. Failure, I suppose, is the closest we come to an admission of sin in a materialistic culture such as ours. And, like sin in the past, failure is punished by shame and with the penalty of exclusion. We fail; we are excluded from the magic circle of success. This is why it is so much more difficult for us today to understand forgiveness and redemption as the central message of the gospel.

The point is not that we should give up trying to complete things. It is very important that we learn commitment, and commitment must always be to wholeness, to completion, to finishing the work we believe in. But what we do have to give up is pretending that we are *in ultimate control* of this process of completion. Details are important. They are the means by which we prove our integrity. How we deal with details reveals exactly the kind of person we are. The way we attend to the small things reveals much more than words or theory. It reveals the state of mind we are in. The very small things in life, the ordinary things we take for granted, like the relationships and routines that compose daily existence, are the trustworthy signals of the kind of state we are really in. But the power that enables us to be committed to wholeness, what is that? What is the power of commitment and where do we find the strength for it? How do we avoid experiencing failure as defeat? How can we avoid responding to failure or sin with that crippling sense of self-pity or despair that leads to premature surrender? Where is the source of power that propels and inspires us to completion, to wholeness, to unity? That power is the actual consciousness with which we live and act.

Meditation is not concerned with details. Yet it has a profound transformative effect upon the details of life and the way we deal with these details. One of the first fruits of meditation is an increased power of commitment to wholeness and completion, to seeing it through, in big as well as small things. But meditation in itself, the actual time of meditation, is not concerned with the details of daily life. It is concerned directly with the purification, the clarification, the deepening and broadening of the consciousness with which we live and which might even be called our Life itself.

It is important however to make the actual periods of meditation part of the details of our life. In other words we have to make the commitment to meditate utterly practical and set aside specific times in specific places. You can think about meditation and agree with its theory and still not do it. Better to disagree with it and do it than agree with it and not do it! Learn to set aside those times with real commitment, real generosity, real seriousness. Two periods a day. It might be more convenient if we could get away with one a day or if we could even get away with one a week or a fifteen-hour meditation every three months. But it does not work like that in practice. You can try it if you like, of course, but part of the advantage of learning to meditate within a tradition is that you do not have to make costly mistakes like that. If you trust the tradition it saves a lot of time. This tradition tells us that every day is a whole. Every day is a unity because it has a beginning and an end. Begin and end your day with meditation – early morning and early evening are the best times – and you are fulfilling that natural wholeness on the spiritual level.

Certainly space the two periods, anyway, at either end of the day and meditate for about thirty minutes. (If you find that is too long at the beginning, you can begin with twenty minutes and gradually extend it). Decide how long you are going to meditate for and commit yourself to that period. Do not shorten or lengthen it arbitrarily. Keep to that time as a discipline. That is why it is very useful to have a little signal to time it. A tape with music at the beginning and end of a stretch of silence, or another kind of signal that will time it for you so that you do not have to be preoccupied by looking at your watch is very useful. Be very practical about those two periods of meditation. Be prepared for failure. Be prepared to find that you lose control of your commitment. You may find that you stop meditating. But do not be defeated by that failure. Just start again.

During the times of your meditation remember that you are not concerned with any of the details of your life. You are dealing with them in a very real way but you are not consciously concerned with them. You are not dealing with your plans, short or long-term. You are not analysing the past. You are not turning over your problems looking for new angles and new solutions. You are not worrying yourself once more with your anxieties, new ones or old ones. You are concerned with deepening your consciousness, with expanding and purifying your spirit. Purifying means unifying. It means training the heart, the centre of ourselves to be more capable of single-minded attention and whole-hearted action. So, when we learn to meditate, we are learning to step aside from the daily flood of details and to step over the constant, roaring torrent of thoughts and images, ideas, fantasies and distractions, with which our consciousness is filled. When you sit down to meditate, do not expect to find yourself instantly concentrated and enlightened. Each sitting is beginning a journey, to where we already are. It is the beginning of a process that does take time but that is also beyond time.

The way to make that journey and to advance that process is the discipline of the mantra, so never lose sight of the mantra. It is all-important to say the mantra throughout each time of the meditation. When, inevitably, you find yourself distracted, do not feel, 'Oh I have failed'. Just simply, gently and humbly, come back to your mantra and start saying it again. As faithfully, as peacefully, but also as determinedly as you can, say it without ceasing.

Our concentration span is very short. It is a sign of the weakness of our consciousness and therefore a sign that it needs to be trained and strengthened. It is always liable to distraction and fantasy through the gravitational pull of the temptation to fall back into disunity, into being scattered in the primal chaos. Kierkegaard warned against what he called 'tranquillising ourselves with the trivial'. It is a good description of much of our society. We are experts at tranquillising and numbing ourselves with what we know to be trivial. When we aimlessly turn on the TV or select the mindless movies we go to, we know it is trivial. But it is a clear choice, to numb and tranquillise consciousness as a means of escaping the burden of incompleteness. Distraction is always asking something new, a new stimulus, as a way of evading the work of enlightenment. In a consumer society we call it variety. It corresponds fairly well to what the Eastern spiritual mind calls multiplicity, the repeated collapse into disunity. Coming to wholeness and unity of consciousness is a joyful but also a serious matter. It is not another activity. It is not one more brand in the variety of distractions. Meditation is not a distraction from life. It is a focusing of life. John Main once spoke about the nature of true religion and said that seriousness leads to joy but solemnity leads to triviality. It is curious how solemnly the trivial in our society usually presents itself. How self-importantly the trivial options of distraction are arranged on the shelves of a consumer's mind!

The mantra is not solemn; meditation is not solemn or self-important. But it is truly serious, and therefore it leads to joy. Joy increases as consciousness is purified, united, deepened. It is a serious work because it is a discipline that involves not only parts of ourselves but our very consciousness, and so the whole of ourselves. When you begin to meditate you may have a little voice in the back of the mind asking you, 'Will I leave this work unfinished as well? Will this be uncompleted?' The answer is 'No', if we can see that it is not only our own work. There is a power working with us on this journey, the power of the Spirit in us. 'The mystery is this,' St Paul says, 'Christ in you, the hope of a glory to come.' The glory is the radiance that we have in ourselves where we are whole. Christ is the proof of this fullness. The face of Christ is completed within us. That is the confidence of meditating in the Christian tradition.

> He it is whom we proclaim. We admonish everyone without distinction, we instruct everyone in all the ways of wisdom, so as to present each one of you as a mature member of Christ's body. To this end I am toiling strenuously with all the energy and power of Christ at work in me. (Col. 1:28–29)

We can begin to meditate with the confidence that the power of Christ is at work in us. We progress by entering the 'knowledge of God's glory, the glory on the face of Christ' (2 Cor. 4:6).

The Word

'. . . and if he should find it, I tell you this: he is more delighted over that sheep than over the ninety-nine that never strayed. In the same way, it is not your heavenly Father's will that one of these little ones should be lost.' (Matt. 18:12)

This is one of those Gospel 'words' that speaks to every human heart and opens it, however closed, however briefly. One of the results of regular meditation is that you hear a 'word' like this and experience not only its wonderful, generous universality but also its amazing application to your own particular life. From time to time it is necessary and helpful to reflect specifically on the connection between meditation and the way we read or listen to Scripture.

Meditation itself liberates in us the unifying principle that helps us to understand where and how this connection is made. The unifying principle itself is the Logos, the Word. As we approach Christmas, each year, for example, we are made more aware through the Readings of the liturgical season of the mystery of the Word, the central reality of the Logos in Christianity. The Word that has existed since the beginning, the Word that is one with God, that reveals God, the Word that *is* God, the Word which became flesh, and the Word who is the Person of Jesus. That is the mystery of Christianity. That eternal and incarnate Word is the core of faith. Christian life, which is generated and nourished by this faith, is the response to this mystery and a progressive penetration of the transcendent and immanent presence of the Word. The Word that is both divine and human is, therefore, fully here, fully present to us and fully capable of being experienced by us. It is no less the Word that is fully everywhere, utterly beyond our capacity to comprehend, in space and time and yet ineffably spiritual. This paradoxical identity of the Word constitutes the core of

114

Christian faith. As we live that faith and, as it deepens and matures, we learn how to *hear* the Word, how to *see* the Word.

As we do so, our consciousness expands by contact with this Word, by that encounter with the Word which is the redemptive and sanctifying experience of life. The human spirit, in meeting the Word, expands beyond the limitations of thought, time and space, all the limitations that we have daily to work with and within. We expand beyond these limitations because we move beyond ourselves. This transcendence and transformation *in this life* is the heart of Christian faith. 'Our minds are remade', says St Paul, 'and our whole nature thus transformed.' Here is the promise and invitation of the Gospel.

We meditate as Christians in the faith that the Word dwells within us, in our heart of hearts. We nourish that faith at other times and in the other dimensions of Christian life with the reading of Scripture and the celebration of the sacraments, which themselves reveal the same Word that lives in our communities of faith, in our deeper selves and in our minds. So, as we grow in faith, we grow through meeting the Word into a unity of mind and heart, into being a unified person and into a single consciousness. As we grow, the *innerness* and the *outerness* of the Word are both necessary for us. A fully developed Christian consciousness unites inner and outer dimensions of consciousness. But when we experience the Word fully, which means when we *listen* to it totally, just as when we say the mantra with complete and undivided attention, there is effectively no inner or outer. These are merely terms of convenience, terms that we have to use within the limitations of our daily levels of consciousness. But when we are fully obedient to the Word, we encounter the Word in *its* dimension of utter transcendence. We are one with the Word when we know that we are beyond inner and outer. We are simply one, and reality is then seen as one with us, one with reality.

This is why there is a profound sympathy between meditation and the reading or study of Scripture. And it is why, for everyone, meditators or not, there are times when we hear the Gospel with a new kind of immediacy and with a kind of insight which is more than clever interpretation. It is a real resonance with the Word that is begotten in the mysterious and eternally unknowable ground of the Father. One of the most perceptible

115

fruits of our meditation therefore is a deeper and richer senstivity to the Word in Scripture.

This is because, as John Main once expressed it, 'we are now approaching the Gospel from an experience of the Word within, the indwelling Presence of the consciousness of Christ'. We begin to read Scripture from within the very same experience of the Word that inspired the writing of the Scriptures. We are entering into that same experience. We begin to listen to the words of Jesus in the Gospels from within his own consciousness. His Spirit calls to mind the words and the consciousness that once formed those words. So we become one with the Word through his words. But the words always point to the Word. The Word dwells in us, 'in our heart', and we listen *fully* to the Word of God when we enter the heart and are most silent. From silence we approach the gospels more attuned, through our own experience, to the spiritual path that the gospels teach and guide us on. The gospels are directed to people who are on or who seek a spiritual journey, who are in the process of having their 'minds remade' and their 'natures transformed'. They are not merely texts for analysis or discussion. Scripture as a whole calls us to conversion, and constant reading of Scripture encourages us to remain committed to the ongoing process of conversion. This same process of conversion is precisely what our meditation is about.

Think of that gospel of the one lost sheep, the one who strayed and who is more precious to the shepherd than the ninety-nine that never strayed. Each of us wants special attention from God. We do not want to be treated just as one more member of the flock, as a speck of cosmic dust. We want to be special, we want to be important in a way that no other sheep is. That wish inhibits each of us but the attempt to get special treatment, or our pique at not getting it, is a veiled attempt at controlling God. There are many techniques of domination or control. Most of them masquerade as obedience or subservience and give rise to the phenomenon of religious egoism, of false humility. As long as we remain within the limits of our consciousness, the limitedness of consciousness being egoism, our motivations are mixed and our sincerity clouded. If we remain within the limits of our consciousness in prayer then we are always demanding special treatment from God for *me*. What I want. What I need. We remain within the limits of desire. Our prayer remains as yet unfreed from egoism as long as we are involved with the activity of the mind in thoughts, words and images. We remain, for example, at the stage of petitionary prayer – asking for new things, concerned with our current needs, concerned with me, with my special needs and the special attention I require.

So, in part, we are using a domination technique, trying to get God to do what we want him to do. Then we are suffering from the great distortion that is known as pride, which is the beginning of sin. The distortion is that we have perverted our uniqueness into separateness. We make the mistake of thinking that, because we are unique, therefore we are separate. Uniqueness then becomes something we experience *only* as separateness. We are indeed unique. We are indeed irreplaceable. And indeed God is eternally and unconditionally concerned with the minutiae of our daily needs as well as with the great events of our lives. The parenthood of God is an essential part of Christian revelation. But the ego-consciousness distrusts this by operating only within its own limits. It interprets this uniqueness as separateness and then tries to protect it. We know the suffering and absurdities that flow from that great error, that great *fall* which leads to the disaster of the tragedy and absurdity of sin. It is what this gospel with a wonderful simplicity describes as 'the sheep going astray'.

The paradox in the experience of salvation is that this is the moment of liberation. It is the moment when we get unique and special attention. Having gone astray we are *found*, having sinned we are *forgiven*. The ego, having been painfully persuaded that separateness is the way to disaster, surrenders itself to undivided consciousness, to the true self, and thereby discovers true personal value. Our value is that we are uniquely, infinitely loved. We go through this process of redemption in many ways and at many times. Indeed we go through it each time we meditate. We die to separateness. We awaken to uniqueness. But it is to our uniqueness *within* the flock who are now our brothers and sisters, equally and uniquely loved in turn. The economy of the Kingdom is not self-seeking, entrepreneurial. The good of each increases the happiness and well-being of every one and of the whole. The wonder of the Gospel is that it reveals the universal and unifying love of the Word for us. The love is already in our hearts.

We are found. The love calls us to fulfilment in this knowledge. It is not a coincidence that it is the *word* of the mantra that leads us to the simplicity, stillness and silence, that allows us to hear the Word.

Stages of Happiness

A little while ago I was asked to hold a baby. As I was holding it I thought I was doing quite a good job of keeping it quiet. It was snuggling in very contentedly. Suddenly from out of nowhere it began to scream and kick. It looked about to bite, so I handed it back to its mother as quickly as I could. As soon as she began to feed it, it became calm, purring with great contentment, perfect happiness. A few minutes later the second child of the family came in. He is about three years old and quite evidently fiercely jealous of the baby receiving so much attention and he set out to get everyone in the room to pay attention to *him*. A few minutes after that, to add to the confusion of the domestic comedy, the third child of the family, who is about ten years old came in, absolutely furious and screaming with anger. He clouted the three-year-old for having broken one of his toys, and the room fell into complete emotional pandemonium. All in all, I suppose, it was a very 'normal' family. Actually, it was a rather unusually happy family.

The children were clearly manifesting different stages of development, different stages of the ego, different stages of desire. These are stages of growth that we all go through, and so they carry emotions that we can recognise and therefore tolerate in children. We even sympathise with them and can find them amusing. They are stages of consciousness that are never completely eradicated as we grow up. They are rather like the rings of growth on a tree. They are imprinted upon us. We all have the baby, the infant, and the angry child still in us. In our more mature moments, or when we succeed in presenting a more mature *persona*, we may doubt this retention of the past and may persuade ourselves we have totally left these behind. In clearer times of self-knowledge we can, how-ever, detect these earlier responses and reflexes in our current

119

behaviour, relationships and responses. Above all it is in our desires, in our satisfactions and disappointments, that we detect a dimension of ourselves where time does not seem to flow, an *aeon* in our psyche where time is motionless and the past has not yet been changed by the future.

These three children represent what we all have within us, a certain reflex of desire. The earlier stages of our development, when we have passed through them, do not immediately cease to exert an influence over us, but have to be gradually absorbed into the later stages. They have to be reconciled with the person that we are becoming; they have to catch up with us. The screaming child in us, however, is not helped to grow up by doing violence to it or by being forcibly silenced; it is helped by being loved into growth by a more mature self. It is in this way that meditation is an essential element in the process of human development. When we meditate we are integrating all the different levels of our consciousness; we are becoming reconciled with ourselves. The first dimension of meditation is always that of our relationship with ourselves, but as we do integrate the personal past, the earlier levels of consciousness, we are deepening our ability to relate with others in a mature and loving way.

Looking at meditation like this is still only to see part of it. If we saw only this facet, meditation would appear to be another method of self-help that is not integrally associated with any spiritual reality or teaching. In our society many, if not most, people begin to meditate without a clear spiritual understanding of the process of human development. But as we meditate something happens. We can indeed begin to meditate motivated by the desire-mode of one of our earlier stages of psychological development, seeing it as a short-cut to happiness, as a way to getting what we want, to fulfilling our desires, to making us safely autonomous. As long as we understand happiness as the product of getting what we desire we will meditate for inadequate reasons. For a long time we continue to equate happiness with the satisfaction of desire because we have still not yet embarked upon the most exciting and most wonderful part of the human journey, which is the renunciation of desire. Beginning this most wonderful stage of development into true happiness, into joy, is what meditation allows us to do. The day we begin to meditate with serious commitment – it may not yet be a perfect commitment and it may indeed take a long time to get into the discipline of meditation – but the day we do begin to apply ourselves seriously, then that day is the eternally repeated beginning of our real journey. As we meditate with simple and sustained regularity – that is what the discipline amounts to – every day and twice a day, then an extraordinary process of awakening begins to unfold. We begin to see, not because we have heard it but because we *know* it, that, as Tolstoy said, 'happiness does not consist in the satisfaction of our desires'. We are not happy because we get what we want.

This discovery is a surprising one and indeed a very deeply disturbing one. It shakes the foundations of our oldest assumptions – the assumptions that we learned as a baby and that were reinforced as the ego grew and hardened and that, indeed, it is the greatest influence of our society to reinforce. It seems almost a truism to a modern post-religious person to say that we are happy because we get what we want. Some TV evangelists of the post-Christian church have no qualms about proclaiming it. Happiness, however, does not consist in getting what we want, because desire itself makes us unhappy. It is the *wanting* that makes us unhappy. The more desires we have, the more unhappy we are. And if there is such profound discontent and pervasive anxiety in our own time, it is because desire and the production of desires, the consumerisation of appetites, has become the major characteristic of our society.

When people are unhappy they often turn to religion, and they can then become deeply disappointed when they discover that religion does not make them happy either. Religious unhappiness produces the great number of functional atheists that masquerade, living and talking, as religious people. Religion fails to lead them to happiness simply because they have been desiring God and to desire God makes him immediately unattainable. There is nothing surprising about that if we look at the analogy with the dynamics of human relationship. On the other hand, to *love* God draws him to us or draws him out of us or draws us into him, whatever way you like to put it. This is why meditation leads to true religion; the word 'religion' meaning literally a re-connection, a re-linking. It is why meditation is a spiritual path, because we are *loving* God, not desiring God, in the purest and the simplest way when we

121

meditate. It is for this reason that when we meditate we are not thinking about God, we are not trying to grasp God or any experience of God. We are not trying to make anything at all happen. We are not thinking about ourselves, either about our happiness or unhappiness.

So what are we doing and how do we do it? We are learning to say the mantra and we do so by listening to it. It is utterly simple. The mantra will lead us to deep springs of joy as it unhooks us from the images that keep us bound to desire, to the patterns, habits and cycles of desire. It springs us free from all images and gradually it frees us from desire itself. It leads to the ultimate felicity of blessedness, if we follow it all the way. One of the problems or challenges along the way is not, strangely enough, the difficulty or the discipline of it but the discovery of the happiness itself. We are not used to being happy, truly happy, for what we habitually identify with happiness is only satisfaction. We know satisfaction when we get what we want and possess it briefly, but satisfaction does not lead to happiness. Meditation however leads to a quite new experience of being happy, even when we do not get what we want, and that is very puzzling for us and very challenging. It makes us ask the disturbing question of where the happiness comes from. Wisdom says that it takes more courage to be happy than to pursue the satisfaction of endlessly receding desire. This discovery is what the New Testament calls acquiring a fresh and spiritual way of seeing. It is about a renewal of heart and mind.

Another stage of development, the final stage, is our becoming fully enlightened by the light of God. Coming to the true childlikeness of enlightenment that Jesus said we have to develop if we are to enter the happiness of the Kingdom of Heaven is the purpose of meditation. If we are to live our lives *now*, rooted in the reality of this Kingdom that is already present in our hearts, we need the courage to meditate each day without desire, renouncing desire: the courage to be happy, to be united with all our former selves.

St Paul spoke of this to the Romans:

I implore you by God's mercy to offer your very selves to him; a living sacrifice, dedicated and fit for his acceptance, the worship offered by mind and heart. Adapt yourselves no longer to the pattern of this present world, but let your minds be remade and your whole nature thus transformed. Then you will be able to discern the will of God, and to know what is good, acceptable and perfect.   (Rom. 12:1–2)

There is no better Christian way of understanding meditation than by these words of St Paul, the worship offered by mind and heart that leads to an integration with ourselves that transforms us in God.

The Need for Failure

The first Christians thought of Christ as the Logos, the incarnate Wisdom of God. Wisdom must always be universal, expressible in the thought and language of every culture. If not, it is not wisdom but merely cleverness, limited by itself. These words of an ancient Chinese philosopher are words of wisdom: 'Empty yourself of everything, let the mind rest in peace. The ten thousand things rise and fall while the self watches their return. Returning to the source is stillness which is the way of nature. The way of nature is unchanging. Knowing constancy is insight. Not knowing constancy leads to disaster. Knowing constancy, the mind is open. With an open mind you will be open-hearted. Being open-hearted you will act royally. Being royal you will attain the divine.'

Lao Tsu here describes wonderfully the process and purpose of meditation. The beauty of those words is their universal truthfulness and their simplicity. Meditation, too, is utterly truthful and simple.

When you are doing a very simple task and you keep failing to do it properly, there is nothing more irritating than to have someone to stand over you telling you how very simple it is. Yet we need to be reminded that it *is* simple, or failure will falsely persuade us that, in fact, it is complex. And, believing that, we will never succeed. Simplicity, complexity, failure. These are all *experiences* that become very real and immediate to anyone meditating. It is better to be prepared for them. To keep these experiences clear and distinct, to be open-minded and open-hearted, we need both to have access to a clear spiritual teaching and to have others to meditate with.

The teaching of meditation is the quintessence of simplicity and clarity. After it has been given initially, to teach it means only to remind. To learn you have only to allow yourself to be reminded. Learning to meditate is not only listening to the

teaching or being reminded. It is the application of the teaching
and a personal bringing-to-mind. It is to return to the source.
This returning is the 'way of nature' and therefore meditation
is a natural way. The practice of meditation leads the meditator
to his own nature. We learn that we possess a common human
nature, sharing it with all other persons. Just as God has one
nature shared by three persons, so humanity, in God's image,
is one nature shared by all human persons. Nothing is simpler
than discvoering this in meditation except the enlightenment
which simplicity leads to, which is unity and union itself.

The purpose of meditation is, however, to let go of these
thoughts and to keep saying the mantra. It may seem rather
baffling to us because we seek our highest values in the purest
realms of thought, but thought is only part of the way. The
complexity we find as we follow this way is in us, not in meditation itself. It is very easy, of course, to project or transfer
our inner complexity on to the teaching. Then we begin to
make a great deal out of the techniques of prayer. How to sit,
how to breathe, diet, reading, décor – all externals – can absorb
us and make us evade the work of simplification. Complexity
always externalises the struggle, but to externalise something
which is really interior is to evade it. It is to run away. Meditation is a refusal to run. It is about acceptance, not evasion.
It is about reception, not rejection. Failure is, not surprisingly,
an inevitable experience for anyone on the way into the spiritual reality. If you do not fail, you will never arrive. You
will never settle into the spiritual reality, which means into
simplicity. If you do not fail, there is no chance of your ever
succeeding. If you do not learn how to deal with failure, you
will never learn how to become humble or, as Jesus said,
'childlike' enough, to enter the Kingdom. Entering the Kingdom means to realise that the Kingdom, the power of God, is
within you, in your innermost being.

We fail in meditation quite naturally; and we should not be
unhappy to fail. We fail in lack of attention; it is strange how
distracted we are, how the very simple task of saying the mantra
is so difficult to perform. All sorts of distractions, all sorts of
feelings flow in to knock us off course and continually bring
about what feels like failure. We also fail in lack of perseverance, especially in the early years of meditation. So it
helps to measure progress in meditation in terms of years rather

than weeks or months. We all fail to persevere. But we fail less often as we persevere. We give up, but we start again.

We probably give up several times because our notion of success is all wrong. Not only are we judging ourselves and our meditation, we are also mis-judging because we do not know what success is. This is because we fail to recognise the true meaning and nature of failure. If meditation were just a matter of mastering a technique, then failure would be final. It would be disaster, with no second chance. You fix a switch, you turn it on and nothing happens – that is mechanical failure. But failure in meditation is not mechanical because meditation is not a technique. The human spirit is not a mechanism. Failure in meditation simply opens the way to a deeper level of experience. It 'opens' the way. It is for us to go through the opening, if we are humble and courageous enough to follow through. If we are too proud to accept failure, we will turn back.

Failure in meditation is like failure in a relationship. An intensification of love, forgiveness and faith will turn the disaster into a wonderful opportunity for new depth. Failure is turned into success in the twinkling of an eye. This is the miracle, not of a machine, but of a living spirit. The miracle of life is rebirth and resurrection. Meditation is the living out of a relationship with life itself. It is the realisation of the simplest, the most fundamental relationship of our life: the relationship with God. But it is this relationship which contains all the other relationships of life and this is why meditation has such a profound effect upon our life. We are not tinkering with the edge of the circle. We are embracing the whole circumference at the centre.

To meditate you need to set aside real time each day, morning and evening. You can see it as an 'investment' of time, or as a 'sacrifice' of time. Either way it is a discipline which transforms our life. The first indication that meditation is about a life-giving relationship is that it leads us directly to the centre of ourselves. This is bound to be surprising and difficult. None of us is exactly what we seem. We know this in relation to others but we also discover that we are not even what we seem to ourselves. The stripping away of illusion, of false images and the emergence of the truth is the reality-dynamic of meditation. This is *what* it is. *Why* should we meditate? If the *what* does not make the *why* self-evident to the sceptic, nothing will.

126

Look at it from another angle. Say that we meditate in order to go through suffering, to put an end to suffering. This is why and what the Buddha taught. It is what Chinese philosphy points to. It is what Jesus makes humanly, universally possible by inviting us to share his transcendence of suffering. That means having to share his failure also. There is no rebirth without the preceding death.

The most frequently given reason I have heard why, in the face of all this, people do not meditate, is that they do not have enough time. It is an extraordinary reason, if you do really agree with the why and the what of meditation or even if you think it might be true. 'I just don't have time.' The very fact that we could think that we do not have time for such a priority shows how urgently we need to begin to make time. It is like saying there is no time to eat or 'I don't have time to breathe'. It is similar logic to the excuse the authorities in Mexico City give for not introducing pollution control measures, that it would slow down economic expansion. We can find many reasons as absurd as that for *not* meditating. The most convincing of all reasons however *for* meditating will be that of our own experience, if only we will take the first step of faith into it. That first step is the liberation of our spirit from the paralysing fear of personal failure and the entry into the universal achievement of Christ.

Simplicity entails practice. It requires the readiness to begin. It means learning not to judge ourselves or our daily meditation, but to begin to keep on beginning. All this is what the Gospel calls faith. It tells us that we will enter the Kingdom of God by faith. The Gospel is the

saving power of God for everyone who has faith . . . because here is revealed God's way of righting wrong, a way that starts from faith and ends in faith; as Scripture says, 'he shall gain life who is justified through faith'.   (Rom. 1:16–17)

127

The Fear of Death

As a rule it is advisable not to talk or be much concerned about any experiences that may happen in meditation, or as a result of meditation. But there is an exception to every rule and I was impressed by the inspiration for many people that came from a description of an experience that someone gave recently to a group of meditators. He has been meditating for several years with the ordinary lack of 'experiences' that accompany the silent, ongoing change in our selves and lives. About nine months ago he was diagnosed as having cancer.

He described how he had first gone to the doctor to be examined, not expecting to hear that anything was seriously wrong. But the doctor had uttered the word 'cancer', the word everyone dreads to hear. It shocked and stunned him. But then, at that very moment, he heard the mantra. The mantra began to sound and it rose in his heart with wonderful peace and certainty. From that moment until the time he was speaking, he understood more deeply every day John Main's teaching that, through the mantra, we learn to hand over control to Christ. He felt every day, more deeply, the presence and the guiding spirit of Christ with him. As he was describing that, I remembered a phrase that John Main used in one of the last letters he wrote, describing his illness and the pain. He ended by saying, 'But it doesn't matter, it is all the Lord.'

The meditator had several operations in a short space of time. After one he lay recovering from the anaesthetic, feeling at the lowest ebb of life and energy he had ever known. He felt utterly powerless, totally weak, as helpless as a newborn child. As he lay there, slowly recovering consciousness, he again heard the mantra. But now, he said, it was not as if the mantra was arising only from his own heart. It seemed to be arising from the heart of all believers. He listened to the mantra as it sounded with a universal resonance and took him into an awareness of cosmic prayer. Then he paused and smiled and said, 'You know, that was the best meditation I ever had!'

What he shared with us is the experience of the mantra as a way that prepares us to be rooted in our own heart and in the universal Spirit who dwells in our heart. This came to him after a long period of faithful meditation. It came to him as he faced death, after he had almost died. Death certainly simplifies us and sharpens our awareness. So perhaps it is not surprising that somebody facing death, unshielded from the fear of death, and entering the total helplessness that we discover in the presence of death, would be open to the fundamental relationship of their existence.

But what about *us*, now? As we wait for that meeting with death, but living as if it would never come. Can meditation now lead us to that same wonderful perception that he knew. Can it give us the certainty, tranquillity and peacefulness, the hope, and courage that it gave him? Can meditation give us this, lead us to this, while we live, not only as we die?

Prayer does give us this if we understand what living and dying really mean. By meditating, by saying the mantra, we are dying and we are facing death every day. And if we face death every day, if we allow ourselves to die a little more each day, then the experience of death will allow us to live each day more fully. Death faced with faith takes us beyond the fear of death and has us live each day with the certain hope of eternal life. That hope is why meditation is a way of life. Because it is a way to die. Death cancels out our sense of the future and so forces us to concentrate wholly in the present moment. Where else is there to go? When we really face death we are totally in the present moment. We enter eternity before we die, if we can face death with this unevasive attentiveness. But we always try to escape the present moment. We usually evade the present, either by living in the past or by creating a world of fantasy. But when we are meditating, the saying of the mantra closes off those two options or escape routes. There is nowhere to go except to be *here*. The mantra points in one direction, towards the centre. It is a narrow path, but it is the path of truth. As we follow the way of the mantra, as we learn to say it with courage and humility, it leads us along a way in which everything in us dies that would hold us back from fullness of life. We die each day in faith and that is the supreme preparation for the hour of our death. But as a way of dying in faith it inevitably brings us to confront two very powerful forces that we must also be prepared to face. They are the forces of fear and of anger.

Whenever we 'smell' death we experience fear, and seek to avoid it. The word 'smell' is perhaps the best way of describing something that is so much part of our animal instinct. As human beings, however, we repress the fear of death because we want to avoid even the idea of it. Repression of fear, though, especially when it is directly challenged by reality, by the mantra, causes anger. All the systems that we have set to maintain repression are activated to resist reality. It is the resistance we experience in our daily meditation. So, great faith is needed to say the mantra, really to sit there and to say it. Not to think about saying it, not to think about our pain or our hopes but to say the mantra. To say the mantra is to have the courage to forget our problems however pressing or urgent. Strong faith is needed to keep saying the mantra through the storms of egoism. But the saying itself deepens faith.

I was talking a while ago with a friend who had been meditating for two years during which, he said, he felt total and utter spiritual failure. He meditated every day, twice a day, for half an hour but he said he never got up from his meditation without feeling that he had totally failed to do anything that he was supposed to do. He could not say the mantra with real attention. Although, he said also, very often, in about the last twenty seconds of the meditation, he began to feel he was about to say it properly just before the alarm went off. But throughout the time of the meditation he felt overwhelming distraction, storms of anger, disturbance and turbulence. So I said, 'What on earth kept you going?' He said, 'I kept going because I *knew* that those times of meditation were the most spiritually fruitful times of my life'. Although those periods of meditation seemed failure he could not fail to see the fruit of them in his daily life. This strange fruitfulness changed his anger at failure into, if not quite yet joy, at least wonder and faith.

The anger that we unearth when we meditate, can, however, often obscure even the sense of the fruitfulness of meditation in ordinary life. It depends how much anger is there, how strong the forces of repression have become, how deep the fear goes. But however much anger is there, when it is released it will distort reality. It will fragment and contract the way we perceive reality. We have to be very faithful to our true vision during those times of distortion. Release of anger leads us to reject ourselves. It makes us very unattractive to ourselves. The anger is in some way eventually turned upon ourselves. But also, unfortunately for those around us, we project it on to others.

In other words anger, and the fear that it springs from, is everything that meditation is *not*. The deepest anger comes from our deepest fear – of death. But it comes from all sorts of secondary causes too, from everything that makes up our psychological history. We need to be aware when we meditate, and as we cleanse ourselves of that anger, that it is not our immediate concern to trace where it comes from. All that is really important is that we are shedding it. What is important is not that we are analysing where it has come from but that we are saying the mantra. What is important is that the love active in the faith of the mantra casts out anger from the heart. We begin to meditate with a great advantage if we start with a developed faith because we begin by being able to understand that anger is cast out by the power of Christ. As we say the mantra we are learning to be rooted in the universal Spirit, the Spirit that Christ has breathed into us, the Spirit by which Christ lives in us. Christ, in the power of the Spirit, can cast out that anger because he is the one who has overcome the primal fear of death and who is now empowered to free us from that fear. Such hope, as St Paul says, brings supreme confidence in living our destiny as vocation. It derives from the Christian awareness that divine love in the humanity of Christ expels all fear:

God is love; he who dwells in love is dwelling in God, and God in him. This is for us the perfection of love, to have confidence on the day of judgement, and this we can have, because even in this world we are as he is. There is no room for fear in love; perfect love banishes fear.   (1 John 4:16–18)

The Cross

The Cross is the supreme Christian paradox. It is the Christian koan, the riddle. And so it poses a question we can only answer if we enter into it. The cross expresses the central paradox of human existence that life only finds its completion, its ultimate fulfilment through death. This paradox is visually presented by the design of the cross itself, in the stark way that two lines intersect, the horizontal and the vertical, the human and the divine. At the point of intersection we find the essential point of reference, the centre for our journey into the fullness of life.

The crucifixion was a historical event. It lasted a few terrible hours. But, because of the unique intersection of the human and divine nature that was contained in the person crucified, the event of the crucifixion transcends time and fills history. The intersection of the eternal and temporal, which releases the power and meaning of the Cross, was not restricted to the individual human consciousness of Jesus. Its influence has entered every human consciousness and is present within each one of us as a living force and a present reality. It could implant itself within every human consciousness, before and after its historical moment, only because of the power of the Divine love which was at work in the Cross through the man Jesus. Only the medium of the purely Divine love could implant it in each one of us because only the Creator's love can love each human being simultaneously, fully, personally and uniquely. Each of us carries the mystery of the Cross within us personally, and so each of us must realise the mystery personally in a unique way. This is what we mean when we say, although we cannot fully understand what we mean by it, that Jesus died for love of each one of us. The mystery of the Cross is that it is both uniquely personal and fully universal. In other words it is both a transcendent and immanent reality. It is full reality,

132

a divine reality but it enters and transfigures the human reality, which is always partial, incomplete.

What was transcended on the Cross? It was the self-limiting, self-protecting force of human consciousness that we call egoism that was crucified. As St Paul says, 'Jesus became sin for our sake.' He took on so fully the transference of egoism from those who, with all the frenetic fear of the ego, rejected his offer of full selfhood, that he who was wholly unself-limiting, sinless, 'became' what he was not. We transcend the last vestiges of egoism in the purifying mystery of death as we become fully ourselves, simply who we are called to be, fully one with the God who is the universal, personal Trinity. The Cross was the total, personal self-abandonment of God, his renunciation of personal existence for us. It became, in the humanity of Jesus, the sacrifice of all human egoism, of mere individuality. The Resurrection is the acceptance of that sacrifice by the Father. That is why the Cross can only be properly understood, and can only be participated in, by the light of the Resurrection. That light is the radiance of the divinised humanity of Christ which burst into being when he completed the cycle of his mission and returned to the Father. The power of his divinised humanity dwells and moves within us, but it is never forced upon us. Love can use no force. It waits, it encourages, but it does not force. This power needs to be seen, accepted, entered. Every meditation and the whole journey of meditation throughout life, is simply the seeing, accepting and entering of this power. It is realised when it is seen, and it is seen when it is accepted and it is accepted when we enter into it. We enter into it as we learn to live continuously in the point of that intersection at the centre of our being. We enter into the paradox, in the way in which it is revealed in each life.

On the Cross Jesus cried out in the anguish of his self-abandonment as he experienced the absence of his Father. The Father who 'abandoned' him remained one with his own self and so the self-abandonment of Jesus was the kenosis of total detachment, though not separation, from his Father who eternally begets him. His cry was the deepest point of human suffering as it attained divine proportion. In reaching that point, however, his human spirit discovered the over-flowing love of the Father for the Son and, in the Son, for all humanity and creation. The absolute presence of the Father to creation is manifest in the union of Christ's spirit with the Father. On the Cross Jesus forgave his murderers because he understood their blindness, their ignorance and hardness of heart. By the integration of those two events upon the Cross – despair and perfect love – Jesus has taught and empowered us to remain in that intersection of the human and divine and to live out of the power of its centre.

The power of the Cross is present in our own centre of being. It dissolves our egoism. It transforms our spirit so that we are able to endure suffering. But if we saw it only as endurance we would not see the Cross in the light of the Resurrection. By that light we are able both to endure *and* to love. When Jesus forgave his enemies, he loved them. He proved to us the most important truth he had to teach, that even absolute suffering cannot destroy the Godlike capacity we possess, which is the capacity to love. He taught us that love is unquenchable and indestructible and even death, the supreme suffering we pass through, does not destroy love. We learn from the cross in the Resurrection's light that all love is divine, a manifestation of God in the human way of being. Therefore, love is a divinisation of Man. These are the lessons we learn not merely by reflection on the Passion but principally through experience of the Resurrection. We learn them through the real events by which the paradox of each life unfolds. As it unfolds we see the simultaneous, present reality of the Cross and the Resurrection as the two poles of our own paradox and so we see the form of Christ taking shape in our life. The seeing is the illumination of our awareness by the invisible and formless Spirit.

As we meditate, we learn to accept the centrality of the Cross in human life. We see it contained but not negated by the light of the Resurrection. We learn to accept the tragedy that every cross is, and so to understand the tragic dimension of each human life and all human existence. As we meditate, we realise that this understanding is the reverse of morbidity or pessimism, because whenever the tragic dimension is embraced it leads to joy. It purifies us, it prepares us, it expands our capacity for existence. What does lead to morbidity, to pessimism and to despair is the attempt to avoid the tragic. I suppose every society has tried to avoid or repress it, but our society, perhaps more than any preceding one, goes to the greatest lengths, with the greatest resources, to suppress the reality of life. We sacrifice the wholeness of truth by enshrining the ego at the centre of life and by spinning the illusion of a deathless earth. Thus we live out of a nostalgia for a long-lost Paradise and fail to enter the Kingdom which replaces and transcends everything lost in the Eden of humanity's infancy.

Meditation purifies us by unseating the ego and taking us through whatever must be endured. It teaches us to have the courage to let the ego die, not to evade death, not to distract ourselves, not to lie to ourselves. It teaches us what the Cross teaches us, that we cannot *possess* any happiness and we cannot *evade* every suffering. If we accept that basic truth, then, by becoming fully empty, we are really filled with the limitless joy of the Resurrection. The liberation of the Cross is freedom from egoism gained in the death of all possessiveness. Meditation roots us in the universal centre, in that personal point of the intersection where we are filled with the energy of the spirit of Christ, his Spirit fully purified, fully realised and fully loved.

> This doctrine of the cross is sheer folly to those on their way to ruin, but to us who are on the way to salvation, it is the power of God. Scripture says, 'I will destroy the wisdom of the wise, and bring to nothing the cleverness of the clever.' . . . Jews call for miracles, Greeks look for wisdom; but we proclaim Christ – yes, Christ nailed to the cross; and though this is a stumbling-block to Jews and folly to Greeks, yet to those who have heard his call, Jews and Greeks alike, he is the power of God and the wisdom of God.   (1 Cor. 1:18–20, 22–24)

Our meditation is our response to the call to take up our cross daily, to identify our death with the dying of Christ which we carry in the mortality of our bodies. Above all it is our response to the call to share in the very nature of divinity which his death and resurrection have opened for us.

When to Let Go

The first time I heard John Main talk about meditation I was moved by how simply he described it as the way to respond to the call of Jesus to 'leave self behind'. If today I had to choose one sentence of Jesus to explain to others why we meditate as his disciples, I would choose that saying of his, 'No one can be a follower of mine unless he leaves self behind.' We have to leave ourselves behind in order to follow him because that is how we participate to our fullest potential in the self-renouncing life of his spirit in which he awakens to the Father. We have to lose our life in order to find his life in us just as he lost his life to find the Father's in himself. Meditation is nothing but the way we do that by letting go of ourselves as we renounce self-centredness, self-consciousness and all self-analytical complexity. We do not *think* about letting go of them, we *let go*.

Sometimes as we follow this way of letting go we are delayed by an inner resistance. We just do not want to let go. Everything we have let go suddenly reasserts itself. At other times we are held back by spiritual doubts or psychological problems. At these moments of trial, when faith is being tested and purified and prepared for a new depth of existence, we touch the human need for a teacher and the teaching. We discover them in the fellowship that we inevitably enter by following the Way.

The strength of a teacher and a fellow-pilgrim is needed, for modern people especially, in facing a very disturbing but common question today: 'How can we lay down our life before we have got it to lay down?' It seems to us, as people shaped by the values of self-fulfilment and self-discovery, that we cannot make any more progress because we cannot lay down what we have not yet got. If we had it we would lay it down happily, but the self still seems incomplete. We do not feel ready to abandon what is only half-formed. The answer to that dilemma is not found so much through arguments or explanations as in gradual, gentle experience. The experience of the union of fellowship answers it because relationships practically teach us that we have to love as fully as we can *now*. We only come to wholeness by giving up what may yet be incomplete. In human relationship we discover the fruit of the paradox that we can and *must* lay down our life continually in order to find it eternally.

At first, it seems to religious people that our relationship with God is the fact of greatest importance in our life. And of course it is, except that it is not a *relationship*. The fact of greatest importance in life is *union* with God. What we name and understand as relationship with God is an image or metaphor. Relationship is a way of expressing the undifferentiated mystery of union. 'Our relationship with God' *is* therefore of ultimate importance. It cannot be neglected or ignored. But we have to understand what kind of symbolic importance relationship has. Its significance lies in helping us to grow into the pure, unsymbolic consciousness of communion. The more fully conscious of the communion we become, the more the notion of 'relationship' as such will be left behind. Our relationship with God is conditioned by time. Our communion with God is free of the limitation of time. Relationship necessarily involves that part of us which is incomplete, still in process of becoming, that personal potency that is becoming the real self. But communion with God discloses the reality of the completed person we are called to be *in* God, who knows us in eternity and chose us before time began.

Personal harmony and happiness, as well as our growth in progressive fullness of being, depends upon finding the right balance in both human and divine dimensions between relationship and communion. That is analogous with the relationship between the spiritual and the religious, between contemplation and action. Balance is something we begin to understand only in the light of ordinary human relationships, and the extraordinary human experience of love as communion. In that light we soon see that balance in our relationship-communion with God, just as with each other, demands detachment. Detachment can only be sustained by stabilised centrality. Experience of human love therefore provides, as John Main believed, the model for the journey of meditation. Loving others teaches us detachment because we learn from human experience that no relationship is final. No 'relationship' is ultimate. The escape from romanticism is a hard lesson to learn. It is even harder to remember and apply in succeeding relationships, but we eventually cannot evade it because human relationships are conditioned by time and, therefore, by mortality. 'The grave proves the child ephemeral' (W. H. Auden, 'Lullaby').

We respond to this discovery either from fear or with courage. Fear tries to persuade us not to enter into any relationship, since we know that they are all subject to the laws of mortality. Whatever we love in time will die. Courage impels us to enter them with detachment. This is the courage of a love becoming always more self-abandoning, because relationships despite or perhaps *because* of their mortality, reveal communion. Death cannot break communion though it fractures all relationships. Death opens an immeasurable void that, like the Cross, reveals communion. It reveals the communion that lies buried deep and runs like a silver vein through the strata of every relationship. In that human unveiling of communion which is love, consciousness awakens and stirs to growth. And we begin to perceive every relationship as living and dying within our communion with God.

Meditation turns us to the divine communion at the heart of every relationship. Detachment, therefore, means an intensification not a diminution, a dilation not a dilution of human love. By the power of silence meditation turns us to the egoless communion at the heart of our self-conscious 'relationship' with God. In that turning we abandon the ego in the detachment of selflessness. We learn thereby the true nature of freedom. We learn (this is both how our life changes and how we learn to love) to let go of relationships even as we form them. This is the practical wisdom that accompanies the grace of living in the present moment. We even learn to let go of our relationship with God by not seeking to possess God. We do so while we learn to let go of the words, ideas and images by which we try to fix and possess objects of experience. We learn to say the mantra. Language and imagination always have a vitalising role to play in relationships but both are transcended in communion where mutual self-knowledge is perfected in silence. So we lose life in order to find it. We lose relationships in order to find communion.

Because of the nature of communion the letting go of the

relationship must be mutual. Both must let go if the communion is to flower. That usually means that one of the two must have the courage to let go first in order to show and lead the way into communion. That is what Jesus has done. He had the courage to let go of himself before us. For us. And so he reveals communion. Our own journey is a creative response, a participatory response. We let go of ourselves both to imitate him and participate in his love and to perfect the communion that he reveals. This is his teaching at the end of St John's gospel:

> It is not for these alone that I pray, but for those also who through their words put their faith in me; may they all be one: as thou, Father, art in me and I in thee, so also may they be in us, that the world may believe that thou didst send me. The glory which thou gavest me I have given to them, that they may be one, as we are one; I in them and thou in me, may they be perfectly one.   (John 17:20–3)

Spiritual Art

Meditation is an art. It is not a science or a technology which we can measure, predict, or run through a computer. It is not a hobby, not something we do just as a pastime. It is not a profession, a career or something for which you have to be qualified. It is an art. What is so remarkable about it is that it is a universal art.

This means that the only requirement needed to practise the art of meditation is our humanity, the possession of a reasonably normal human consciousness. No special genius or skill is demanded, only the obvious precondition that we want to meditate. We also need a very down-to-earth disposition: to want to meditate seriously enough to persevere in the art. In weekly meditation groups around the world people are introduced to the tradition of meditation. In the teaching from our Benedictine Priory in Montreal they meet it as part of the monastic tradition, but it is essentially universal to the Christian understanding of prayer. No particular group or strand of the Christian tradition can claim it for its own. It is important, however, to learn to meditate within a spiritual tradition. Modern attempts to despiritualise meditation and reduce it to a physical skill or psychological technique fail to lead people beyond the first elementary stages. They lack the transcendent power of art.

The most important aspect of the weekly groups, after introducing people to the practice of meditation, is that they actually meditate together. Practice is infinitely more important than anything that might be said about it. Practising within a tradition brings the tradition alive, vitalising the word with the Spirit. Every time we come to meditate, the depth of silence and the quality of stillness is the real context of learning, of being taught by an ancient tradition. Meditation is an art we have ultimately to learn from experience. One of the great

140

teachers of meditation in the early days of Christian monasticism even said that 'experience is the teacher'. After the meditation at the weekly groups people have an opportunity for questions or discussion if anyone wishes. At times people will have much to raise and talk about. But, probably more often, they will feel that the silence has expressed something no words can. The stillness has moved them on further than they were. The most important part of any religious or spiritual meeting like the most important part of learning to meditate, is the actual time given to prayer. I was recently asked to take part in an interfaith day of discussion. The organisers had so far excelled themselves that the dialogue left no time for meditation together, the one thing we could have shared at the greatest depth. It seemed to me that as a result of this bureaucratic coup, what had been achieved in talking would have no really enduring importance. In a few days the waters of activity would again cover that small island of communion we had touched. If we had made time to meditate, the achievement of our dialogue would have been preserved, not merely on paper or tape, but in our spirit, the living tablets of the heart.

Like any art, meditation requires dedication. Dedication means practice. Most artists frequently suffer from the great temptation that overwhelms everyone from time to time. It is the inclination to dream his creation, to daydream about the next work, to plan his next creative endeavour but to postpone the practice until the end of the long dream. This tendency to become a postponing dreamer is very strong in us all. It is as strong in us as the ego. It can become so strong that the dream can seem real. Dreams usually seem utterly real while they are being dreamt. And so with a certain amount of help from the Society of Dreamers that feeds the distractedness of our world, we can deceive ourselves that we are *doing* what in fact we are only *thinking*.

For spiritually minded people, and I suppose most readers of this book would be likely to accept that description, this illusory practice is a special kind of danger. If you are building a house and day-dreaming about how beautiful it is going to look and postponing the actual work of creation, it will not be long before somebody comes up to you and looks at the empty site. They will say 'You are talking a great deal about this house, but I don't see anything there.' It will then be difficult to maintain the self-deception that you are in fact building the house. Being awakened from a dream like this is not pleasant at first. On waking, most people are not their best selves, rather grumpy and impatient. On being shown the empty site our first reaction may well be anger. You can equally well be day-dreaming about your spiritual life, building an imaginary interior house, speculating about self-knowledge, fantasising about the way you will soon become seriously committed. Spiritual day-dreaming can become much more prolonged than other kinds, because it may seem to others, looking from the outside, that you are making a real dedication of time to working on your spiritual life. The voice that eventually awakens you from spiritual day-dreaming may take a long time to penetrate.

But there are times when we know that we are not day-dreaming about our spiritual journey. These are the daily times of the mantra. The signs of this real practice in our external life will be gradual. They are more subtle, more pervasive, than the signs of physical or intellectual growth, becoming fit, building a house or learning a language. We know that we are progressing spiritually from deep changes taking place in ourselves: a freeing from fear, the deep fears that we always ran away from or suppressed, a lifting of anxiety that seemed to be endless and causeless, an ending to loneliness, a new-found capacity for solitude, a new zeal for creativity, a sense of joyfulness in the ordinary things of life, and above all a new spirit of love. The external signs of these changes unfolding deep within us only become conscious gradually and subtly. As we meditate we become less self-conscious and therefore less self-analytical. And so, the paradox of growth in meditation is that we become less immediately or self-consciously aware of our progress *as* we progress. We experience growth more through contact with others than by thinking about ourselves. We come to know more about ourselves from the knowledge that other people have of us than from our own introspection. We begin to be teachable by experience. When you think of this kind of new consciousness and way of relating, you see that it means living in a new world: a universe very different from the self-analytical and self-obsessed cell from which we start the journey.

But having said that, there are two simple ways which do make progress easily visible. They are two ways in which we know that we are actually on the spiritual path, that we are not day-dreaming, that we are not fooling ourselves. These two ways together constitute fidelity to the discipline of the art of meditation. Firstly, we are saying the mantra with as much fidelity as we can, from the beginning to the end of each meditation. Nothing could be simpler than that, nothing could be more real than that. Secondly, we are meditating every day, twice a day, each morning and each evening, as regularly as we can. Those are two self-evident signs, daily verifiable and unmistakable, that we are not day-dreaming and are in fact waking up, becoming conscious. It is only necessary to be reminded periodically of the discipline of the art. That is why people meet together to meditate, to strengthen an absolutely simple discipline. Complexity issues from illusion. And there is no limit to the complexity that follows compromising on simplicity and which we compound by postponing our awakening.

The fuel for the journey is the power of silence. At first it may seem that it is the power of will. But as we proceed, and to proceed is to progress, we realise that the real power is greater than our will. Silence is an experience which we may have to wait some considerable time really to know. It is not just the absence of words. When we have stopped talking, we are still employing – or employed by – the language of the imagination. When we have gone past images we still face the abstract language of thought, of ideas and concepts. The experience of silence lies on the other side of all these dialects of the language of consciousness. The mantra guides us through the words, the images and the thoughts, and all the complex compounds that are created by their interraction. It leads to a space and a time within, where at first there seems to be nothing. But it is out of this apparent nothingness, out of silence, that the fullness of being comes. Our completeness is made in meeting the Being of God. And in the silence of God's Being we encounter the one Word that is Logos. It is God's language, one word that expresses everything of his fullness: the Word of God that is Christ's humanity.

On the way to this silence, and even as we arrive, we are always learning to listen. If meditation is an art, it is the art of paying attention purely to the mantra. The best way to describe how we say the mantra then is that we *listen* to it. We go

143

through every level of being as we travel the route to our heart where we find silence in the Word of God. This is what is always demanding about the discipline of meditation. But in comparison with what we find and with what we are given, even as we travel, the discipline is child's play. If we can learn to be like a child, the discipline itself will be delightful. We have to learn to say the mantra, but this means to leave behind our worries and fears, even our sadness. To leave that behind is not escapist but redemptive. With a generosity of spirit that gives everything we are to that simple, loving act of saying the mantra we teach the heart to sing. At first, it requires concentration and a certain effort. But later as we learn the art, the best way to see it is not as concentration but as attention through stillness. We can however only begin to learn if we begin to practise. Remember, it is a universal art. And as we follow the discipline as Christians, as disciples of Jesus, we discover the universality of Christ. We discover that universality to be in our own particular hearts.

When in former times God spoke to our forefathers, he spoke in fragmentary and varied fashion through the prophets. But in this the final age he has spoken to us in the Son whom he has made heir to the whole universe, and through whom he created all orders of existence: the Son who is the effulgence of God's splendour and the stamp of God's very being, and sustains the universe by his word of power. (Heb. 1:1–3)

In meditating with Christian faith we listen wholeheartedly to the Word of power God has spoken to us in the Son. The greater our depth of listening, the further we expand beyond our narrow self-sufficient worlds into the universe of God's Being.

Ignorance or Unknowing

A survey was recently held in several European countries to test the general knowledge and political sense of the average person. The results were revealing about the special characteristics of the different nationalities. The level of knowledge was in general rather low. But when the English did not know the answer they pretended not to care. The French refused to admit that they were wrong. The Irish refused to admit ignorance by changing the subject or by claiming that the question was wrongly phrased.

Reflecting on this, I am inclined to think about the nature of knowledge and the way we idealise knowledge without distinguishing it from information. One of the character traits of our society is the enormous importance we attach to knowledge in the unprocessed form of raw facts and figures. We are inundated with such knowledge. However trivial, we pursue the instant food of data which has become readily available but which is also overwhelming. No one mind can possibly hope to absorb it all and the explosion of knowledge as information has consequently had a major effect on the meaning we give to education. Education is now seen primarily as a way to gain access to and acquire mastery of knowledge. It is a way to power and success, to influence and status, because whoever can handle the tool of knowledge is a master not a slave. How true this is, is another matter. But it is what the information-culture is conditioning us to believe.

Wittgenstein complained forty years ago that modern education was more concerned with putting information into people than with teaching them how to learn or think. Today it is less information itself than access keys to information banks that education is concerned with. Education and raw information, misnamed knowledge, have become commodities, something that can be acquired, bought and sold, as a business.

This limited sense of knowledge about the world is a deeply engrained feature of our society and conditioning. And, therefore, it is not merely external to us. Each of us is at least partially trained or conditioned to respond to knowledge as if it were merely information. Even self-knowledge or personal knowledge of others has a tendency to be reduced to what can be reported or quantified. Ever since the computer became a tool of the Freudian mind it has been almost impossible not to think that we know more about ourselves or others by retrieving forgotten or repressed information. The problem is that there *is* a real degree of truth in this discovery. Or rather, the problem is that we think this is *all* the truth. Knowledge *does* require information and thrives on it in the early stages of consciousness. But beyond a certain point we need to learn another and simultaneous way of knowing, that forgets or renounces information. The way of wise ignorance, the way of unknowing we call meditation.

Anyone who begins to meditate today does so conditioned by these influences. We are unconsciously tempted to think of 'spirituality' as another way of knowledge, a way to break into the God-programme, to gain and amass knowledge as information about the spiritual realm. Spirituality itself has even become a commodity. Glossy magazines advertise new brands, conventions and committees spawn bureaucracies. I recently heard of a spirituality centre subtitled 'a holistic learning organisation', which offers courses such as The Spirit of the Celtic Guitar, Native American Basket Weaving, Yoga Training for Athletes, Meditation and the Art of Japanese Flower Arranging. In fact when you read the course descriptions they are so enticingly presented you really feel you must take the course to learn about these things if you are to be complete, to be whole. Especially – there is this hint – if you want to be *more* complete and whole than your neighbour. However, the enthusiasm and erudition of much 'New Age' spirituality should not be overshadowed by its excursion into gnosticism or commercialism. The main religious traditions also should be stimulated by the intensity of the spiritual hunger felt by so many non-aligned people. The danger and the opportunity are equally great.

We face, at several important crises on the journey of meditation, the problem of confronting this cultural conditioning personally and of understanding how this external situation has been internalised. It is the kind of conditioning that makes us think, unconsciously perhaps, of meditation as a 'course', as something we undertake to get more information, to get experience. If it gets demanding we can simply give up and transfer our energies to a new enthusiasm. When it gets difficult it can seem that we have exhausted it, 'for me anyway' and that there is no more to learn from it. In fact we have perhaps then come to the point where we have most to learn, where knowledge ascends through information to unknowing. Confronting a materialistic and grossly ego-centred conditioning in the spiritual life will not be amusing. It will be painful and demanding and it may even make us at times fearful. And perhaps the deepest fear is of entering a state of ignorance. Knowledge, or what we think of as knowledge, is so highly placed in our system of values that unknowing is an ignorance that seems a terrifying unreality. Knowledge we value so highly that we want to acquire, possess and control it, is demonstrable, measurable, recordable – facts that we can see. By contrast, the spiritual knowledge of meditation seems like sheer, valueless ignorance, sheer foolishness. It is entered by unknowing the demonstrable and measurable knowledge of information as we let go of all that can be seen, measured and recorded. In its place we enjoy not facts but faith, an invisible reality, the 'knowledge of things unseen'.

We fear ignorance because of the letting go and because we associate ignorance with shame, with vulnerability, with danger to ourselves or our identity. Knowledge makes us safe, unknowing is a risk. Meditation requires both the simplicity of a child and the courage of an adult because it leads us to a place of no-knowledge, a place of unknowing which is a point of poverty of the spirit. When we can really grasp that the ignorance which we are entering as we meditate is poverty of spirit, then we have passed the most dangerous part of the journey. This is the stretch where we might turn back. But when we have passed it, when we know enough *not* to turn back, where we have enough faith not to turn back, then we will begin to mine the treasures of the vein of poverty. At first we may say, 'I have earned something more than this. I deserve something more than poverty and unknowing.' We need to remain here, apparently learning nothing, doing nothing. By the standards of our social conditioning we are merely wasting time. Yet here, in this place of poverty, we acquire faith and discipline. We are strengthened by the discipline. The moment comes when the poverty begins to be revealed to us as a source of unfathomable riches, but only when we have been strengthened by faith and when we have enough discipline to engage in its revelation. We then encounter a power infinitely delicate, and elusive if we try to know, possess or record it. We encounter our own spirit which is our own true self-knowledge. Self-knowledge is itself. It is the knowledge that cannot be known or used by any knower. It retreats again as soon as we try to know it. As soon as we try to capture it we relapse into self-consciousness. The spirit is free and cannot be captured.

But even then we must keep moving. We must learn continually to unlearn the self-knowledge that we gain. To be poor is to be faithful and to persevere in practising the renunciation of self right down into the depths of our selves. We keep saying the mantra. Then in an ever new poverty we encounter our spirit again but now in the spirit of Christ. We know ourselves, now, in Christ, in and part of his self-knowledge, his Spirit. This is only a beginning. It is the real beginning of the Christian journey hidden in every act of faith, and it is the essence of meditation as a Christian, because we enter into union with the Spirit of Christ. The knowledge that is now ours is quite different and far superior to the knowledge that we once thought so valuable. We know, above all, in a different way. We now know because we are known and are allowing ourselves to be known by the Spirit of Christ. We are coming to know, as he knows, that his spirit is the Spirit of the Father and the Son, the self-knowledge of God. In this lucidity of knowledge, the knowledge of the unified consciousness, the usual rules of knowledge owe obedience to a higher logic, the Logos. The self-importance of the usual kind of ego-based knowledge becomes painfully evident. We now enter a realm of mystery in the experience of paradox, and understand the traditional oxymorons: luminous darkness, fruitful sterility, wise ignorance, grand poverty. At this point we know that the most important thing there is to know is that we are on the journey, that we are faithful, that we are *in* Christ who described himself as 'the Way'. He described his life as a returning home to the Father, and meditation becomes simply our sharing that journey with Christ. In learning to unknow, the meaning of the Scriptures becomes stronger:

'Believe me when I say that I am in the Father and the Father in me; or else accept the evidence of the deeds themselves. In truth, in very truth, I tell you, he who has faith in me will do what I am doing; and he will do greater things still because I am going to the Father . . . If you love me you will obey my commands; and I will ask the Father, and he will give you another to be your Advocate, who will be with you for ever – the Spirit of truth. The world cannot receive him, because the world neither sees nor knows him; but you know him, because he dwells with you and is in you. I will not leave you bereft; I am coming back to you. . . . The one who has received my commands and obeys them – he it is who loves me; and he who loves me will be loved by my Father; and I will love him and disclose myself to him.' (John 14:11–12, 15–19, 21)

Hope

When they first begin, most people expect that meditation is going to solve all their problems. As experience teaches us what meditation is really doing, we come to understand that the daily work of the mantra is doing something else and something *more* than solving our problems. This is difficult for us to get our minds around, because it asks for a new way of thinking from us. We just want our problems solved; we do not want to be bothered with the details. But the generosity of God is greater than our needs. Redemption gives more than the Fall took. God gives us more than we can ask. In receiving more than we either deserve or even desire, however, we are challenged to transcend our notions of rights and needs. We are summoned to a wholeness that leaves nothing of our selves out. Whatever is repressed must be released. Whatever is hidden must be made clear. Every detail has its place of meaning and we are called not to passive but active receptivity. Meditation is actually restructuring our life. This is how St Paul in the first Letter to the Thessalonians describes it in words that are among the first recorded words written by a Christian:

> We always thank God for you all, and mention you in our prayers continually. We call to mind, before our God and Father, how your faith has shown itself in action, your love in labour, and your hope of our Lord Jesus Christ in fortitude.   (1 Thess. 1:2–3)

The restructuring of our life to a new wholeness is empowered by the three great virtues of faith, hope and love. Those first words of Christian teaching have come down to us to show us today, and every generation, the essential structure of Christian life. I would like to look at one of those virtues in the light of the experience of daily meditation. The three form one indivisible reality and we can only separate them analyti-

150

cally. We cannot separate them existentially. In the Christian life we live them all or none. We live one with the power of the others. But in some ways hope is the most interior and, in a sense, the most personal of those virtues. St Paul says that faith shows itself in action and love in labour or work, hope shows itself in fortitude.

Hope is the inner disposition we see only in its influence on perseverance. In an analogous way the Holy Spirit, who is traditionally associated with hope, is the Person of the Trinity we never see. The Father is imaged in the Son, and the Son sends the Spirit. But the Spirit has no image. Although the most interior, and so the most invisible, and with the least definable external signs, hope is no less than the others a virtue that can be shared. When we sense hope in another person it gives us hope. For some reason deeper than reason, meeting hope in others gives us the strength to be strong, to persevere. In our own time perhaps the greatest and most urgently needed gift that the Christian can give to the world is the gift of hope. A society begins to deconstruct, just as a psyche begins to lose the harmonious power that holds it together, when hope weakens. But hope is a gift that can only be given through experience, not in theory. Giving hope is more than being spiritually hearty and trying to buck up failing enthusiasm. It is not by talking about hope but by being hope-full that we transmit it.

John Main liked to distinguish between hope and 'hopes'. We may have all sorts of hopes for the future but many of these hope-wishes have to be let go of if we are to experience pure hope – the essential Christian virtue of hope. Hope is more than optimism, which is a healthy but not very contagious virtue. When we see optimism it often tends to make us rather pessimistic. Hope is much more than just temperamentally looking on the bright side. We can be hopeful when – perhaps only when – all hopes have been disappointed. Hope can shine out from the midst of total disaster. We can and must be hopeful at the moment of death. Hope is not a desire for anything. It is not day-dreaming about anything. It is the reverse mode of fantasy. Hope is a fundamental attitude or direction of consciousness. It is an outward turning to the self, from self-reflection to the contextual reality in which it finds itself. To be hopeful is to make the discovery that we are integral parts of something greater than ourselves, and that we are living with the energy of that complete reality. Hope is the outward turning of the self, whatever the difficulty of remaining outward-turning. Despair is the surrender of consciousness to the force of introversion. Beyond a certain point it is, humanly speaking, irreversible and leads to symbolic or actual self-destruction. It is important therefore to keep constant surveillance on the force that leads to loss of hope. Regular prayer continuously contains it. We need similarly to watch others who are in danger of losing hope and to 'catch them' before they get to the brink. Hope is an absolute, constant and unconditioned virtue. You cannot be hopeful only when things are going well. You need to be hopeful and, in a sense, to *choose* to be hopeful, however things go, whatever the inclination to sink back into self-consciousness, into the safe enclosure of the ego.

Hope is one of the virtues resulting from deep prayer. It is in deep prayer that we turn from self to God, the God who is 'other' than ourselves but to whom we bear a likeness more striking than to our family or any human being. Hope is the aspiration to be totally at home. It is the strongest aspiration of our being. The word 'virtue' means 'strength'. The virtue of hope is a strength of spirit. But to be virtuous does not mean only to do the right things and be a respectable person. To be virtuous means to be strong in the Spirit, to have accepted the gift of the Spirit's strength. Strength comes from our realising our likeness to God; the strength that helps us persevere, grow, be faithful, loving and hopeful. We grow in strength in areas that we often do not recognise at once. Often we remain fixated in awareness in areas of familiar weakness such as impatience, intolerance, desire, vanity and so on. It is part of the hopelessness of our age that we are so fixated upon human weakness. We are intensely aware of the lack of health in the psyche, the mind, or spirit, but so often unaware of the strength that is constantly being given to us and the whole human race through our common human nature, now linked to God in Jesus. We can therefore be blind to areas where we are actually growing stronger.

Hope is a silent virtue. It is not shown so much in action, or 'work' as St Paul says, but in fortitude or, as another translation puts it, 'patience'. If hope has a sign it is not stubbornness or inflexibility but gentle patience. We can be unaware of growth in hope precisely because it manifests itself by its own nature and over time. You may find after a week that you are more loving, but a week is a little too short significantly to prove you are more hopeful. To recognise growth in hope needs the dimension of time. The other virtues are more associated with the dimension of space – what we see and touch. But when we see the development of hope, when we have enough time and experience to look back through the lens of the present moment, we enjoy a wider and deeper vision of the transformation that meditation is working in our life. We see the restructuring of life by the co-operating powers of the three virtues. Hope, that helps us to persevere, leads us to vision.

We may look to see where this hope has come from. Why are we more hopeful? Why have we persevered in meditation when we gave up on so many other things? The Latin word for hope, *spero*, suggests the word *spiro* which means 'I breathe'. Both suggest the word *spiritus*, spirit. Hope is a virtue breathed into us by the Spirit. As we detect its presence in our life (detecting it is part of our growth in self-knowledge) we have an opportunity to accept a revelation. It is the revelation of the mystery of the Christian God, because we are offered the opportunity to recognise the Trinitarian character of Christian prayer and indeed of the Christian life. The Holy Spirit is operative in life through experiences that are often the most elusive and most difficult to define. They are experiences that span the spectrum of life, and the quality of these touches of the Spirit is the most pervasive. Take the experience of love, for example.

Love requires a certain degree of hope to be born. A despairing person cannot see or respond to the opportunity for love. But love also magnificently stimulates the blooming of hope and expands to cover the whole of consciousness during its most intense moments. To be hopeful is to be conscious of the Holy Spirit in our life. To be hopeful is to be inspired, which means to have a continual 'in-spir-ation' of the Spirit going on within us. Living in hope means to enjoy the continual breathing of the Spirit into our life. This is the prolongation of that specific moment when Jesus breathed on his disciples as he appeared to them after the Resurrection. It is this breathing of Jesus, and of the Holy Spirit, into us which is the gift. Hope therefore implies gratitude. The gift for which we are eternally thankful is the gift of the prayer that never ceases. The continuous saying of the mantra leads us into this prayer which is like the continual in-flow of pure energy into a system that has lost its ecological balance. We regain the purity of being, we remember our basic goodness, through the pouring into our hearts of this pure love of God, the Holy Spirit that Jesus sends.

If you have ever been to Niagara Falls you will remember the terrific power of the falls as they crash down. If you have stood at the point where the water falls, you may have noticed how extraordinarily still it is at that point, almost like glass. The stillness of our meditation is rather like that point where the infinite power of God falls into us, floods our inmost heart empowering and transforming our lives.

This is the power of the new age of the Spirit which the New Testament acclaims:

> You are on the spiritual level, if only God's spirit dwells within you; . . . if the Spirit of him who raised Jesus from the dead dwells within you, then the God who raised Christ Jesus from the dead will also give new life to your mortal bodies through his indwelling Spirit . . . For all who are moved by the Spirit of God are children of God. The Spirit you have received is not a spirit of slavery leading you back into a life of fear, but a spirit that makes us children, enabling us to cry 'Abba! Father!' In that cry the Spirit of God joins with our spirit in testifying that we are God's children. (Rom. 8:9, 11, 14–16)

The Necessity for Solitude

I think most meditators have had the experience at least once of sitting down, starting to meditate and then feeling an almost uncontrollable urge to jump up, turn on the TV, get a drink, write a letter, go for a walk, make a phone call, read the newspaper, have a sleep, do anything, except meditate. What that experience suggests is that as we are put in touch with our real self, we also encounter the disquieting experience of solitude. If we try to be faithful to the mantra and to the discipline of the twice-daily periods of meditation, then we can be certain that meditation will lead us into solitude. And as solitude is a quite unfamiliar quality of existence to us, when we meet it in this way through meditation, it can disturb, even panic us. Many people claim to long for the opportunity for solitude. A few of these make or take the opportunity when it arises. Of these a very few are prepared for the suddenness of the disillusionment or for a life without distractions, for being themselves with themselves. Perhaps people meant for total physical solitude are even rarer than those meant for total physical chastity. But a degree of solitude, like a degree of chastity, is a spiritual necessity for everyone who would be whole.

Solitude attracts us because it seems to be the path we are searching for: simple, no-nonsense, not a head-trip, not somebody else's experience, direct. It is the path to the centre that we long to find, to the true self and the source of all personal value and meaning. But it challenges us because it is not the escape that we thought it would be, the getting away from it all. By this point we have probably tried many ways of getting away from it all and discovered their sham-ness. From time to time we are tempted to try them again, to jump up from the solitude of meditation and try to get away from it all.

Yet it is quite different, this experience of solitude, from loneliness. In loneliness we *do* get away from it all: and that is the problem. We get away from everything. We retreat into complete alienation, even from ourselves, our true self, the centre and spirit of our humanity, and so away even from life. The experience of solitude, into which meditation leads us if we have the courage of simplicity, is not an escape. It is an encounter. The great mystery that unfolds to us the more wonderfully the more we are still and enter this new world of being, is that this encounter happens at a level of being where we thought there was no one to meet. At a level that we avoided because we did not want to find ourselves and realise the fear of being ultimately alone, there we find everything we have been looking for. And once we did everything to distract ourselves from ourselves because we were so frightened to discover the eternal, cold loneliness of the self! But meditation reveals that fear as the ultimate foolishness, because at that level of our being where we thought there was no one to meet, we meet Christ.

If meditation traces the path to fullness of life, if it is a path that makes the whole of life a journey into full humanity, and if meditation involves this essential experience of solitude, then solitude must be an element of human fulfilment. It is important to understand why this is so, if we want to become more conscious in our relationship with Christ, if we want to understand the Christo-centric dynamic of the way of meditation.

The fullness of our humanity resides in the ways we realise our relationships. The way we fulfil all the relationships of which we are capable, and which life is meant to discover, fulfils the unique network of relationships that form the pattern of the identity and destiny of our true self. This is so crucial that we should waste no time. We should do everything we can, as our first priority, to transcend the egoism, the intolerance or the fear that destroy relationships. Meditation shows its connection with Reality, not by any superficial phenomena, nor by any trivial experience that may happen in meditation itself; this is why it is so important to remain detached from everything that happens in meditation. Meditation, rather, shows its effectiveness in the way we make relationships. It leads to a deeper and sharper awareness of our true nature. The truth of human nature is not, as we dread it is, that of an isolated speck of cosmic dust, a lonely monad, but that we are beings in communion. At the deepest centre of our being, where we have not yet been, where we have not yet become conscious, we are in relationship, in love. Communion is the essential potency we enjoy and it is what we live in the hope of fulfilling. The closer we come to this essential gift of human being, the potency for communion, the fuller our hope and our joy.

As we approach it, the experience of solitude must be embraced, because solitude is the encounter with the decisive acceptance of our own uniqueness. It is the total opposite of loneliness. Loneliness is the escape from, or the suppression of our uniqueness. Meditation leads into solitude and so it empowers us for deeper and truer relationship because the fundamental relationship is the accepting of our self. The more we are in conscious touch with our own self's uniqueness, the more we can relate in depth and reverence to the real person in others. The extraordinary Christian paradox appears here, in that we need other people to help us pursue the journey into solitude. We need their human love, their compassion, their understanding and intimacy. This is a neglected aspect of why the Gospel tells us that without human love anything that we call the love of God is a farce and sham. The challenge, then, that solitude presents us with is a happy difficulty because it creates communion.

But there is pain involved also, because as we enter solitude our relationships change. At whatever point we begin the journey of meditation we have a certain network of relationships. The most extreme recluse cannot escape relationships altogether. At whatever point the journey into solitude is begun, it influences the relationships we have at that moment. The experience of meditation begins to deepen and to change those relationships, as well as preparing us for new, perhaps broader and unexpected relationships. A major change in the pattern of relationships we have, and in the way we make new relationships, is initiated silently, because we are gently required to give up dependencies. The dependencies of our emotional life are the relationships with people or things that appear to console us in loneliness but actually reinforce our loneliness.

At the beginning, most relationships are made at the level of egoism which begins to develop in infancy. The primary relationships that are first formed there create a lifelong pattern. They imprint themselves upon us. They programme us.

As long as we stay at this level we continue to make relationships with the means offered by the level of egoism, and we find ourselves repeating the same patterns. We can come to feel like a needle that has got stuck. There are new situations, new people, but the same pattern, over and over again. All relationships are still being formed by the energy of egoism and so they are fearful. And so, as fear expresses itself in anger, they frequently become aggressive. Dependency always creates fear whether it is the fear of loss, the fear of being possessed, the fear of having to possess others, the fear of responsibility. The fear of the ego intensifies as it realises it is inadequate for the responsibilities of real selfhood.

Meditation changes our relationships because it changes *us* by leading us out of the level of egoism, out of its too thin atmosphere. We begin to breathe the purer air of the self and to see further and more clearly into other selves. Meditation leads to the level of spirit, the true self; and the relationships that are made with the energy of this level of being are relationships of love. They grow with less and less fear, less and less dependency, more and more power to liberate and fulfil. Everything depends upon that transition from the level of egoism to the level of spirit and, for that, everything depends upon the courage with which we will let go and encounter the true self.

As Christian disciples we are fortunate to be able consciously to encounter a person who has transcended the ego and, persevering in that meeting, we enter into a relationship formed by the pure energy of his spirit. This relationship with one more whole, more centred in the spirit that we are, is a relationship with a teacher. In Christ we find the supreme teacher, and we are each of us fortunate because each of us has the call to encounter him as the living human being who has no longer any ego at all. To encounter such a person is to be led directly into their heart, a heart without egoism, a chamber without walls filled with the light of love. This is the journey we make when we meditate, as we enter into relationship with Christ.

The first great discovery of the early Christians, awaits each of us today.

So now, my friends, the blood of Jesus makes us free to enter boldly into the sanctuary by the new, living way which he has opened for us through the curtain, the way of his flesh.

We have, moreover, a great priest set over the household of God; so let us make our approach in sincerity of heart and full assurance of faith, our guilty hearts sprinkled clean, our bodies washed with pure water.   (Heb. 10:19–22)